D0537770

ADVANCED POKER

ADVANCED POKER

RULES, SKILLS, TACTICS AND STRATEGIC PLAY

A COMPLETE STEP-BY-STEP GUIDE TO MASTERING THE GAME,
WITH MORE THAN 400 PRACTICAL PHOTOGRAPHS AND ARTWORKS

TREVOR SIPPETS

southwater

This edition is published by Southwater

Southwater is an imprint of Anness Publishing Ltd
Hermes House, 88–89 Blackfriars Road, London SE1 8HA tel. 020 7401 2077; fax 020 7633 9499
www.southwaterbooks.com; info@anness.com

If you like the images in this book and would like to investigate using them for publishing, promotions
or advertising, please visit our website www.practicalpictures.com for more information.

UK agent: The Manning Partnership Ltd
tel. 01225 478444;
fax 01225 478440;
sales@manning-partnership.co.uk

UK distributor: Grantham Book
Services Ltd
tel. 01476 541080;
fax 01476 541061;
orders@gbs.tbs-ltd.co.uk

North American agent/distributor: National Book Network
tel. 301 459 3366;
fax 301 429 5746; www.nbnbooks.com

Australian agent/distributor: Pan Macmillan Australia
tel. 1300 135 113; fax 1300 135 103;
customer.service@macmillan.com.au

New Zealand agent/distributor: David Bateman Ltd
tel. (09) 415 7664; fax (09) 415 8892

ETHICAL TRADING POLICY
At Anness Publishing we believe that business should be conducted in an ethical and ecologically sustainable way, with respect
for the environment and a proper regard to the replacement of the natural resources we employ.
As a publisher, we use a lot of wood pulp to make high-quality paper for printing, and that wood commonly comes from spruce
trees. We are therefore currently growing more than 750,000 trees in three Scottish forest plantations: Berrymoss (130
hectares/320 acres), West Touxhill (125 hectares/305 acres) and Deveron Forest (75 hectares/185 acres). The forests we manage
contain more than 3.5 times the number of trees employed each year in making paper for the books we manufacture.
Because of this ongoing ecological investment programme, you, as our customer, can have the pleasure and reassurance of
knowing that a tree is being cultivated on your behalf to naturally replace the materials used to make the book you are holding.
Our forestry programme is run in accordance with the UK Woodland Assurance Scheme (UKWAS) and will be certified by the
internationally recognized Forest Stewardship Council (FSC). The FSC is a non-government organization dedicated to promoting
responsible management of the world's forests. Certification ensures forests are managed in an environmentally sustainable and
socially responsible way. For further information about this scheme, go to www.annesspublishing.com/trees

Previously published as part of a larger volume, *The Complete Practical Guide to Poker and Poker Playing*

Designed and produced for Anness Publishing by THE BRIDGEWATER BOOK COMPANY LTD.

Publisher: Joanna Lorenz
Editorial Director: Helen Sudell
Project Editors: Polita Caaveiro and Dan Hurst
Designer: Simon Goggin

Cover Designer: Simon Daley
Art Director: Lisa McCormick
Photography: Andrew Perris
Production Controller: Pirong Wang

PUBLISHER'S NOTE
Although the advice and information in this book are believed to be accurate and true at the time of going to press, neither the authors
nor the publisher can accept any legal responsibility or liability for any errors or omissions that may be made.

CONTENTS

Poker Strategy

The various poker games that have developed over the past two centuries have given rise to many theories regarding poker strategy. To an extent, many of these are extrapolated from the mathematics behind the game, since with a single deck in use there is always a finite number of possibilities at work, however large. Yet poker is played by and against people, which gives rise to a host of other factors that have to be taken into account when assessing the chances of winning a hand, securing a profitable session, or emerging triumphant from a tournament. The style of the game being played, the betting structure in operation and the stake levels applicable will all influence a player's decisions, as will the characteristics of the opponents themselves. This chapter focuses on the five standard forms of poker, high-only, and outlines some of the key factors that newcomers and experienced recreational players alike must consider if they are intent on improving their poker-playing skills.

Right: A player commits his remaining chips to the pot by betting 'all-in'. This move is a familiar sight to those who have seen poker on television, which almost invariably features no-limit Texas Hold 'em, a game in which players may risk all their chips on a single hand whenever it is their turn to bet.

DRAW POKER

Draw poker begins with all players contributing an ante to the pot. Working clockwise, the dealer deals one card at a time face down until each player has five cards. The option to open the betting falls upon the player to the dealer's left, but only if holding a hand that has a pair of jacks or better. If not, the option moves around the table until someone with a qualifying hand commits chips to the pot. After the first betting round, players may discard up to three unwanted cards and replace them with others from the deck. After the draw, a second round of betting ensues, the first player to act being the player who opened the first betting round. If two or more players match bets in this round, the game ends with the showdown when they reveal their cards to identify who has the winning poker hand. The pot may also be claimed if, during either the first or second round of betting, a player makes a bet and the opponents all fold.

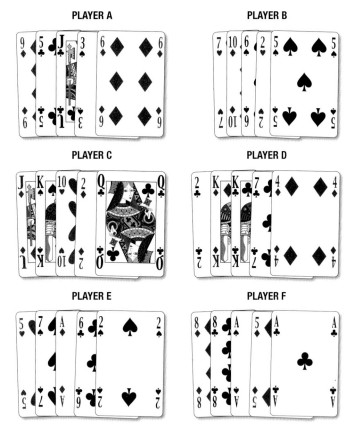

PLAYER A **PLAYER B**

PLAYER C **PLAYER D**

PLAYER E **PLAYER F**

Above: A typical range of hands after the deal in a six-player game where player A is dealer. Players B and C cannot open the betting since their hands do not qualify, but player D can with the pair of kings. A two-card draw for a flush is unlikely to be successful, so player D should keep the kings and discard the other three which are not high enough. Player E has no pair and should fold. Player F could raise any opening bet and take the pot now with two pairs, aces up. A call is safe, as the odds are against anyone improving enough to beat the hand. Betting should prompt players A and B to fold but player C could call to draw one card to a straight – either an A or a 9 will do.

As the original poker variation, draw poker was initially played as a no-limit betting game, which made it suitable as a gambling medium for the wealthy and those who possessed an uncanny ability to bluff. The imposition of limits on the betting broadened the game's appeal, while the adoption of rules governing who opened the betting for each hand further transformed draw poker. With the advent of jackpots, the variation in which a player who opens the betting must possess a pair of jacks or better, draw poker became a much more mechanical game that rewarded sound strategic play. Although still popular in California's card rooms, where for nearly a century it has been the only poker game permitted by law, elsewhere, draw poker has diminished in significance compared to seven-card stud and Texas Hold 'em. Nevertheless, the game provides a solid foundation upon which beginners can gradually expand their poker knowledge, it being the first form of poker most people learn to play. Online poker sites that feature draw poker host games without the requirement for opening the betting with a pair of jacks or better. As such, this deprives players of one of the elements essential to formulating a strategy, namely the certain knowledge that one opponent holds at least a pair of jacks. For this reason, attention here will be focused on jackpots, the draw poker variation that invokes the opening requirement and in which the draw is limited to three cards.

Starting hands

In order to have a clear concept of a good starting hand, it is necessary to contemplate what is ultimately likely to win in a full-handed game of six or even seven players. Anyone dealt two pairs or better in their first five cards immediately possesses a hand that has about an even-money chance of winning without improvement. Two small pairs might prevail, but combining a pair of aces with a lesser pair is preferable. This is because the hand has only an 11 to 1 chance of improving to a full house, assuming a one-card draw, so anyone not holding a pair of aces is vulnerable to opponents who draw two cards to a pair with an A kicker – the highest unpaired side card in that player's hand. They have a 4 to 1 chance of achieving two pairs – with aces up – or better, leaving an opening hand of two low-to-medium pairs as the likeliest to be leading before the draw but trailing afterwards. Holding a pair of aces presents a player with a 3 to 1 chance of improving the hand after a three-card draw and wins frequently enough in its own right to warrant support, particularly in a light betting heat. Pairs lower than jacks are considered risky propositions when calling the opening bet, since such a hand is evidently already trailing. Anyone holding a higher pair has the same chance of improving as the player with the lower or underpair. So a three-card draw to a pair of nines, for example, has a 3 to 1 chance of improvement, generally speaking, and a 7 to 1 chance of becoming three of a kind, known as 'trips'. Yet such improvement may still leave the hand second-best at the showdown, a prospect that is even more likely, given that the opener will occasionally have much better than a pair of jacks.

Seeking information

Players who have developed an understanding for the game soon recognize the inferences to be drawn from the bets made by opponents. Although up to a fifth of all deals may feature no hand good enough to open, when a player does possess such a hand, there is a strong likelihood that another is in circulation. Should the first player to the dealer's left choose to open the betting, taking the earliest position or acting 'under the gun' as it is known, then it is fair to assume that a pair of aces or kings is the minimum hand being advertised. Players opening with anything less in an early position find it hard to justify calling a subsequent raise, since they are almost bound to need improvement on the draw. In mid and late positions, players are inclined to open with jacks or queens, but will also be wary of anyone who then raises. Such aggression would signify the raiser probably holds at least a pair of aces, and more probably two pairs or three of a kind. In a fixed-limit game, raising with less than a pair of tens is hardly worthwhile, since it is difficult to bet a sufficient amount to prevent the opener from calling with what is, by definition, a better hand. Only a tight player known for only raising with rock-solid hands might perpetrate a successful bluff under such circumstances, underlining the importance of understanding one's opponents and their playing styles.

Above: When dealt two pairs, such as the jacks and eights shown here, a player has an even-money chance of winning even if the hand does not improve. Discarding the 6d in an effort to draw an additional J or 8 for a full house is a logical move, though the odds are against the full house.

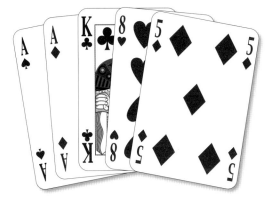

Above: Being dealt a pair of aces offers a player the chance to open the betting in any position, even when first to act. But if an opponent should raise an opening bet, they are likely to be holding two pairs or better. So, if choosing to call, the player holding this hand will probably discard the 8h, 5d and hope to find a K or another A to be in with a chance. There is also the possibility that both cards drawn could be a pair to go with the aces.

Above: Whether to play a pair of queens will depend on a player's position at the table. If the option to open has been checked around to a player in late position with this hand, a bet is advisable, if only to collect the antes. If an opponent raises, the player holding the queens must expect to be losing, since the opponent is likely to have at least a higher pair and possibly more. Calling with a fairly good hand is one of the consistent features of the game.

Betting clues

Prior to the draw, the only clues available regarding any player's hand come from the betting. Those with an early advantage will normally bet to emphasize it, the one exception being when a player holding a 'pat hand' – an outwardly strong hand since he or she opted not to exchange any cards at the draw – calls the opener, rather than raising, to encourage others to do likewise and boost the pot. But with only two betting rounds, it is usually best to press home an advantage by forcing opponents either to fold or to inflate the pot in their own efforts to find a winning hand. In a fixed-limit game, therefore, although a player with an average hand – a low pair, perhaps – may call the opener and trust to fortune, anyone who subsequently raises is unlikely to be bluffing. To raise with less than a high pair, which could be vastly inferior to the opener's hand, invites disaster when players need only call one more bet before the draw. Pursuing this strategy will virtually guarantee heavy losses in the long run, since the pot odds will rarely match the odds against securing a winning hand. In other words, when successful, the chips won will not compensate for those lost in the inevitably frequent defeats. Players who favour pot-limit draw poker have a little more scope for a speculative call and the occasional bluff, but in order to beat the odds they will normally have to read their opponents exceptionally well.

Playing the draw

Deciding how many cards to draw after the first round of betting is often straight-forward, particularly if the betting itself has offered a few clues as to the potential strength of opponents' hands. Understandably, it is sensible to draw the number of cards needed to

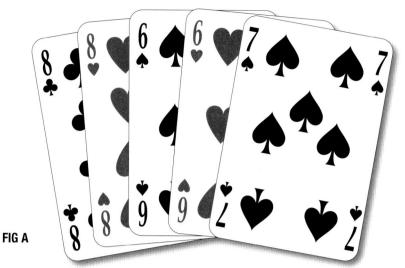

Above: When contemplating how many cards to draw, players need to balance the likelihood of improving sufficiently to win against the cost of obtaining more cards. Holding two medium pairs prior to the draw puts a player in a probable winning position, but it is 11 to 1 against drawing to the full house that would make victory almost certain.

Above: Players who hold four-card flushes have a 5 to 1 chance of completing the hand, but the one-card draw should only be contemplated when there are several callers in an unraised pot.

Above: Any players hoping to draw two cards to complete a straight are trying to beat odds of 22 to 1, making it a speculative play, at best.

maximize the chances of securing the best hand possible, although there is an exception to this rule when a player holds three cards of the same value, also known as 'trips' – a potential winning hand even without improvement. Two-card draws to straights or flushes are rarely worth considering, whether playing a fixed-limit or pot-limit game, while one-card draws for the same hands are best played cheaply against several opponents. The possibility of some vigorous betting in the second round makes the implied pot odds more attractive in this situation, especially as the hand is likely to be a winner if it hits. Against just one opponent, drawing one card to a straight or flush is much less appealing, since the odds of reward rarely justify the risk. To improve upon two pairs requires drawing one card for a full house, but the odds against this occurring are an unattractive 11 to 1. This is why players holding two pairs usually raise the betting in the first round to drive out weak hands and reduce the chance of being outdrawn.

As mentioned earlier, a player holding trips is best advised to draw one card, as opposed to two, even though this reduces the chances of making a full house. Such a move disguises the value of the hand and makes it more likely that an opponent will call a second-round bet with a losing hand, having assumed, wrongly, that the player possesses two pairs or is bluffing with a busted straight or flush. If an opponent decides not to draw further cards or 'stands pat' as it is termed, then anyone holding trips will definitely draw two cards in the expectation that a full house may be necessary to win. Players who are dealt pat hands of a straight or better can usually assume they are in a winning position, leaving them free to concentrate on building the pot.

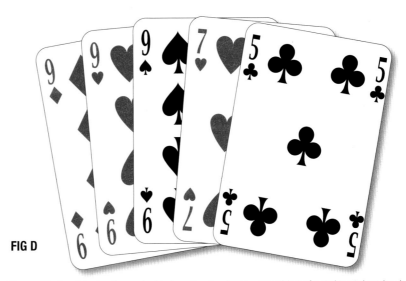

FIG D

Above: Finding 'trips' – three of a kind – after the deal is something of a rarity, and such a hand is a regular winner. Rather than discard the two odd cards in a bid to improve the hand, it is often worth a player retaining one to help disguise the hand's real strength. Opponents may read a one-card draw as indicative of an attempted straight or flush, or that the player holds two pairs at best.

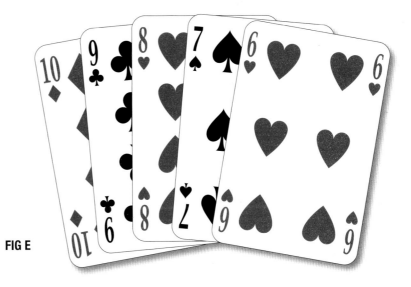

FIG E

Above: While holding trips is beneficial, being dealt a pat hand such as a 10-high straight should safely see a player claim the pot; extracting the most chips possible from opponents then becomes a matter of pot management.

Observing opponents

Apart from the information to be gleaned from bets made in the first round, the draw is the only other point in the game when players may gain an insight into the hands held by opponents. Remembering how many cards were drawn and by whom can provide clues to the value of hands in competition for the pot. Discounting an outright bluff, anyone choosing to stand pat with their original five-card hand is obviously confident that they possess a probable winner. Otherwise, players typically draw as many cards as necessary to give themselves the best chance of improving their hands. Those making three-card draws are almost certainly retaining a pair, the value of which can be reasonably estimated if the opener opts to do this. Two-card draws suggest trips or a pair with a high kicker – the highest unpaired side card in that player's hand – since drawing two for either a straight or a flush will bring success on fewer than 1 in 20 occasions, making this an unattractive proposition to most players. Finally, players who draw a single card are perhaps the most difficult to read, since they could be holding anything from a currently worthless four-card straight to a virtually unbeatable four of a kind. Generally, it is best to assume that a player who opens or raises the betting and then draws one card probably has at least two pairs and maybe even trips. In an unraised pot, players drawing one card are more likely to be trying to buy a potentially lucrative flush or straight as cheaply as possible.

Right: Following the opening bet, players A and D fold, but the remainder all call for 25 chips. The fact that no opponent raised could indicate several things: they may each hold a pair that was too low with which to open, leaving them a 4 to 1 chance of improving past a pair of aces; or they may have four-card straights or flushes that they are hoping to fill. At least one opponent may have a powerful hand and be trying to build the pot.

THE DEAL

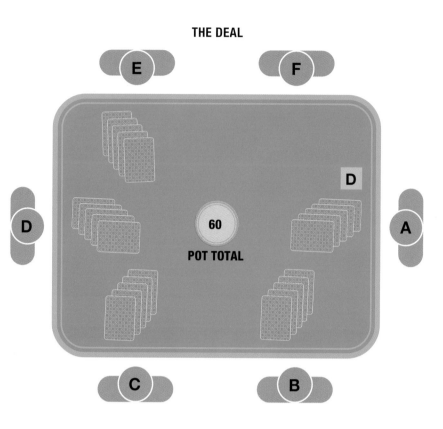

PLAYER F

Above: This example hand of a 25/50 fixed-limit game highlights some of the likely thought processes facing a player throughout a typical game. After the deal, the option to open the betting is checked – or passed – around the table until player F, holding a pair of aces, bets 25 chips. On the assumption that nobody is slow-playing a stronger hand, this high pair may even prove good enough to win without any further improvement.

THE BETTING

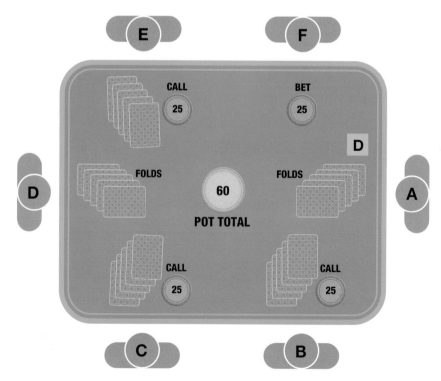

Above: Having opened the betting and indicated that he has at least a high pair, player F keeps the J kicker to disguise the value of the hand. Opponents are then forced to consider that player F may well hold three of a kind. Had the Jc been discarded as well, it would be clear that player F holds a high pair and no more.

Odds against

Players who prosper at the game are generally well versed in the probabilities applying at the deal and before the draw. The odds of being dealt a pair of aces or better, for example, are 8 to 1, which emphasizes the need for patience while waiting for a playable hand, as even a pair of jacks and above will only materialize once in every five deals. Against five opponents, a pair of aces has a better-than-even chance of being ahead, which makes it worth playing in most cases. At the other extreme, receiving at least a straight directly from the deal will occur once in every 132 occasions, underlining the rarity of a genuine pat hand. To put this into perspective, a six-player game could see the deal circulate 22 times around the table before anyone is dealt a straight or better. Of the other key opening hands that offer good prospects of winning, two pairs or better will happen once in 13 deals, while a hand of at least three of a kind will appear once in every 35 deals.

ON THE COME
♦ ♣ ♥ ♠

Any player who draws cards to a hand with potential rather than to a hand that is already made is said to be 'on the come'. The term can apply to players with two pairs, for example, who may draw one card to try catching a full house but, in a game where two pairs is often good enough to win, such a holding could be described as a made hand already. It is more usually associated with four-card flushes and straight draws that need one more card to complete the hand. In the best of such situations, namely holding an open-ended straight flush draw, the odds against hitting any one of the 15 cards that will complete – or fill – either a straight or a flush are 2 to 1. At the other extreme, needing one card for an inside straight draw is 11 to 1 against being successful, odds which preclude anything but a cautious betting approach.

THE DRAW

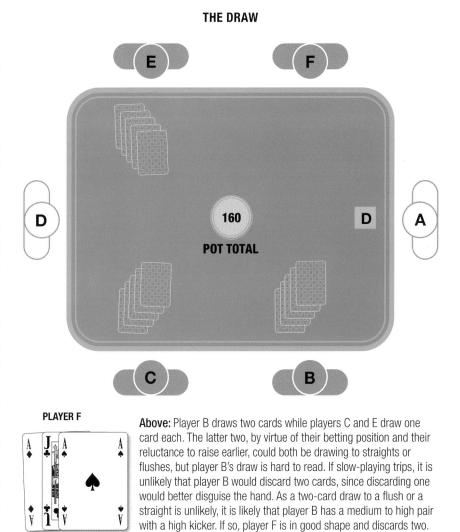

PLAYER F

Above: Player B draws two cards while players C and E draw one card each. The latter two, by virtue of their betting position and their reluctance to raise earlier, could both be drawing to straights or flushes, but player B's draw is hard to read. If slow-playing trips, it is unlikely that player B would discard two cards, since discarding one would better disguise the hand. As a two-card draw to a flush or a straight is unlikely, it is likely that player B has a medium to high pair with a high kicker. If so, player F is in good shape and discards two.

Pursuing value

Only by comparing the relevant pot odds with the chances of improving a hand sufficiently to win can players ensure that they bet in support of good-value propositions. In fixed-limit games, the implied pot odds before the draw rarely exceed 3 to 1, less than the chance a player holding a low pair has of beating an opponent holding a pair of aces. Opportunities to bet when the pot odds are in favour of drawing a probable winning hand are therefore rare in a game where players with weak hands sensibly fold, leaving two or possibly three players to contest the pot. Players holding a four-card straight or flush are definite underdogs against just a couple of opponents and will be unlikely to win a pot sizeable enough to justify the risk of playing. The situation changes when the opener has several callers, since more bets can be anticipated in the second round, thus increasing the pot odds. A one-card draw to a flush or an open-ended straight has a 5 to 1 chance of completing the hand, which makes this a much more attractive proposition in a multi-handed pot.

Following the draw

Betting strategies following the draw are dependent on several factors as players try to assimilate the various strands of information obtained so far. A player opening in early position is advised to bet again in the second round only with an improved hand, otherwise a check is recommended. Anyone who is already beaten will not call a bet, while those who have improved to a possible winning position will call or even raise, perhaps prompting a call from the opener that simply compounds the loss. In fixed-limit poker, the cost of calling is rarely enough to make bluffing in the second round a serious option. Those bluffs that are successful tend to be set

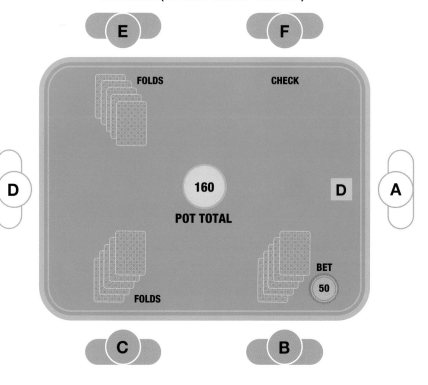

THE DRAW (SECOND-ROUND BETTING)

PLAYER F

Above: As the opener, player F has the option to act first in the second round but, having seen no improvement following the draw, the only sensible option is to check. When player B bets 50, player F immediately has doubts that the pair of aces is still strong enough to win, since, if reading player B's hand correctly, it is only 3 to 1 against it having improved from one medium pair to two pairs or better. This would make the bet justifiable in terms of the available pot odds, while a bluff in this situation is unlikely.

Right: A player theatrically tosses his cards away to indicate that he is folding, even though there is a massive pot at stake. Folded hands should always be added face down to the 'muck', this being the pile of discarded cards that accrue during the play of each hand that is the responsibility of the dealer.

up with a strong pre-draw bet or raise, a move that could be enhanced by subsequently not drawing any cards, or 'standing pat' as it is otherwise known. Another general rule is not to bet with anything less than a premium hand, an A-high flush or better, for example, when one or more opponents have drawn one card without previously having raised the pot. Anyone who completes a straight or better will raise any second-round bet, while those who missed their hand will inevitably fold.

Straights and flushes

Holding a straight or a flush, especially A-high, puts a player in a strong position, as such hands can be expected to win, or hold up, on most occasions. How the hand is played after the draw will depend on the circumstances beforehand.

If a made flush is dealt to a player who then opens the betting, then another bet in the second round is almost obligatory. Players who have improved to three of a kind, for instance, may call just to be certain that the opener is not bluffing. Checking merely allows players who fear they have not improved enough to check too, and this reduces the potential winnings.

If an opponent opened, then there are other possibilities for a player with a pat straight or flush. A call will probably keep other players involved, but a raise is not out of the question if the game is loose with plenty of action. When a player successfully draws to a straight or flush, calling the opening second-round bet is generally a sound policy. Those players whose hands remain inferior despite having improved, may well be tempted to call, or perhaps even raise, in the face of perceived weakness. A raise at this point, however, will probably eliminate players who would otherwise call and, once again, reduce the potential winnings.

Above: A player raises the betting by adding more chips to the pot. The raise is an aggressive move, of course, and usually indicates possession of a strong hand although this perception allows players to employ it as a bluffing technique too. When choosing to raise, players should announce their intention clearly before committing their chips to the pot. Adding sufficient chips to call the previous bet and then announcing a raise is known as a string bet and is not permitted.

THE SHOWDOWN

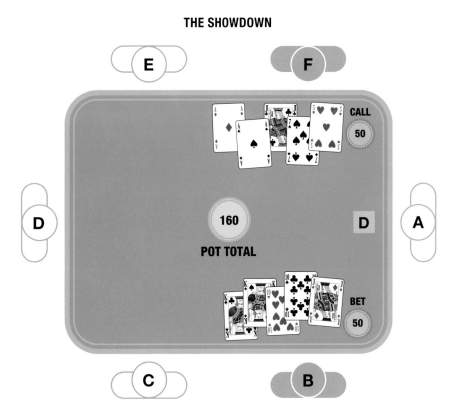

Above: The fact that players C and E quickly folded suggests that they completely missed their draws, leaving player F to decide whether the pot odds, now 4 to 1, justify calling player B's bet. In the event, player F does call, suspecting that player B may hold a lower pair than aces, which did not improve. At the showdown, player B is the winner, but player F's earlier check is vindicated. A bet would surely have been re-raised by player B, meaning that player F would probably have contributed 50 more chips just to confirm defeat.

FIVE-CARD STUD

The pattern of play for five-card stud permits from two to ten players to engage in a game which begins with each player contributing the ante to the pot before being dealt two cards, the first face down and the second face up. The player with the highest-ranking face-up card, otherwise known as the 'door card', opens the first round of betting with a compulsory bet known as the bring-in, following which opponents may fold, call or raise. When the first round of betting is completed, those still involved in the game are dealt a third card, also face up, and a second betting round follows. Again, the player showing the best hand opens the betting with this honour quite often falling to a different player in each round as successive cards are dealt. The game continues with a fourth face-up card being dealt, followed by another betting round and then, if necessary, competing players receive a fifth card face up as a prelude to the final betting round. As ever, the winner is decided either at the showdown when those still involved reveal their hands or by a player making a bet at any stage of the game that is not called by opponents.

Five-card stud represented a major departure from draw poker, the first recognizable form of the game. Although the introduction of betting limits and restrictions on which player opened the betting expanded draw poker's popularity, the paucity of information available upon which to base any betting decisions led to the development of open poker, of which five-card stud is the oldest surviving example. Open poker games are those in which several of the cards in each player's hand are exposed for all to see. In five-card stud, each player ultimately receives one card face down and four face up, if participating to the fourth and final betting round. The structure of the game therefore enables players to modify their strategic thinking after each successive round, as more cards are exposed and the inferences behind opponents'

Below: This is a typical scene after the final card has been dealt. Three players have survived the first three betting rounds and the action is on player F who boasts the best visible hand, a pair of aces. This could be enough to win but, since player A has obviously called on fourth street when both opponents were already showing open pairs, it is possible that player A has a concealed 9 and has successfully completed a J-high straight. This would be enough to beat the others who can only hold three of a kind at most.

As they appear to the opposition   **As they appear to the player**

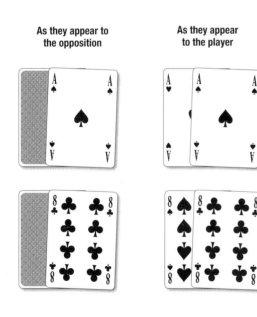

Above: To be dealt a pair in the first two cards usually provides a player with an immediate advantage, although high-ranking pairs are obviously of more value since they are more likely to win the hand without any improvement required. The odds against being dealt any pair are 16 to 1, but seeing queens or better in the first two cards will happen around once in every 74 deals, while receiving a pair of aces is a 220 to 1 chance.

TYPICAL FINAL-ROUND SCENE

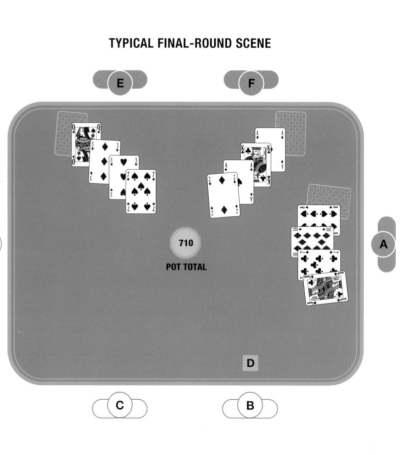

betting patterns become more apparent. In addition, since there is no draw to put pressure on the deck, five-card stud can accommodate up to ten players, which is the number of participants considered ideal by experienced players and poker professionals. Such a game is likely to create betting confrontations that are essential to an enjoyable session. Adopting a pot-limit or no-limit betting structure will also help to counteract the mechanical facets of five-card stud that are prevalent in a conservative fixed-limit game. Bluffing becomes a more attractive possibility when bigger bets are permitted and the pots can escalate sufficiently to tempt players into staying with hands that might usually be folded in a fixed-limit contest.

Starting hands

In common with all poker variations, judging which opening hands to play and which to fold is the first important element of five-card stud. After the deal, this decision is based upon the receipt of just two cards, of which one is visible to opponents. This might initially seem to present a player with too little information upon which to decide whether to fold or play, but an understanding of the odds affecting the game emphasizes why this decision is important. Any player who stays to the showdown has an even-money chance of obtaining a pair. In a six-player game, therefore, if all players see five cards the likelihood is that three of them will possess at least a pair, with one of these likely to be queens or better. Possessing a pair of aces or kings gives any competitor an advantage, and the earlier that pair materializes during play, the better. The ideal situation is to be dealt a pair in the first two cards, since a player in this position can exercise more control over the betting. When holding two unmatched cards, the general advice is to be cautious and fold immediately, unless both cards are ranked 10 and above. The only exception to this rule is when a player has a hole card, one that is held face down on the table, that is higher than any door cards (the first exposed or 'up' card) on display. A player can expect to see a pair of aces once in every six deals, so an A in the hole with a 7 showing, for example, presents a player with a fair possibility of making the high pair. If this occurs and there are no other aces or open pairs among opponents' up cards, then the hand has a good chance of winning at the showdown, supposing the player is unable to force opponents to fold beforehand by betting aggressively.

Above: A pair of queens, often referred to as 'ladies', is a strong opening hand in five-card stud. After the deal, a player holding a pair of queens should expect to be leading since only a pair of aces or kings could be beating the hand at this stage. If there are no door cards higher than a Q on show, then the player will be aware of holding an immediate advantage.

THE VALUE OF PAIRS
♦ ♣ ♥ ♠

The value of being dealt a pair in five-card stud can hardly be overstated. Although possessing a pocket A or K to match the door card is desirable, even lower-ranked pairs can be valuable to some extent. In a tight game where players are exercising caution, a raise from a player showing a 7c, for example, may cause the opener and any callers holding higher-value door cards to fold, for fear that a pair has already been secured. After the deal, a six-player game presents any player with odds of just over 3 to 1 against pairing the high card in this situation, odds that worsen considerably if one of those cards is dealt to an opponent. That unfortunate situation may be enough to induce conservative players to fold. Whether one is dealt a pair or not, in a high-stakes or no-limit game of five-card stud, bluffing with a big first-round bet to suggest a pair is a plausible tactic. However, it is rarely considered by players holding unpaired cards, either of which is ranked below a 10.

Door cards

Before the first round of betting takes place, the first exposed or 'up' card dealt to each player – the door card – offers the only clue as to the potential of each hand. The player with the highest-value door card opens the betting, but this obligation may fall to a player holding a 7 or an 8 on occasion, in which case several callers can be expected. If the door cards are low, it increases the chance that players will have high-value hole cards – those dealt face down and thus unseen by opponents – which could encourage them to stay in for a round or two. A raise from a player showing a low door card normally indicates a pair is held, and a similar assumption may be wise if the player merely called the opener.

Social players are not always aware of the probabilities at work, so the skill of the opposition needs to be considered when seeking a link between the exposed cards and any bets. Poker is a gambling game, and many players are prepared to pay over the odds for the thrilling, if unlikely, possibility of making a powerful hand.

Likely winning hands

As suggested, the average winning hand in five-card stud is much lower than in other poker variations, with a high pair usually being enough to claim the spoils. Finding such a hand within the first three cards is an advantage, particularly if the pair includes the hole card, as it offers the chance to raise the betting and drive opponents out of the pot. In doing so, many hands with the potential to win will often be folded before they are complete. For example players who hold three-card flushes or straights will hardly ever encounter the pot odds to make it worthwhile to continue with the hand, especially when an opponent has an open pair. Such hands are rarely seen, while even three of a kind has only 1 chance in 35 of being dealt in a

OPEN PAIRS

Left: Three examples of hands after the dealing of the third card face up – third street – all showing an open pair. Typically, the minimum bet for the first two rounds in five-card stud is half that of the last two rounds. Any player holding an open pair on third street, however, is entitled to protect it by doubling the minimum bet, making it more expensive for opponents to try beating the hand. If choosing not to exercise this option, any opponent not showing a pair may also bet at the higher level, if desired.

Below: Workers playing a game of poker in 1940 at the Fort Blanding site, Florida, used by the US army as an infantry replacement training centre during the Second World War. At least eight players are involved making it likely that five-card stud will be one of the poker variations considered for the evening's entertainment. With more cards in circulation the chances of players formulating good hands is increased, thus helping to make the betting action much more competitive.

player's five cards. Since a hand this strong may not materialize until fifth street, the prospect of having to survive three rounds of volatile betting in order to achieve it underlines why hands of such magnitude are seen so infrequently. By contrast, it is difficult to capitalize on trips being held in the first three cards dealt, since the open pair that must be apparent compromises the chances of keeping enough opponents involved in the pot to make the hand pay off.

Third street

The receipt of the third card – third street – marks the decisive point for most five-card stud hands. Good players will rarely consider going beyond this stage if their hand is outranked by an opponent's visible face-up board cards in play. They adhere to the primary rule, which is that any player who cannot beat the board should fold as a matter of course. An example occurs when an open pair appears, the recommendation being, for any player not yet holding a pair, to fold. Having cards that rank higher than an opponents' cards on the board – also known as 'overcards' – might seem worth playing, but pairing one of these could prove inadequate, especially if several other players stay involved. Sometimes, the opponent showing a pair will already have three of a kind and anyone in this position will happily entertain speculative calls from the unwary.

Sensible third-street play precludes betting in support of causes that may already be lost. This applies to hands such as three-card straights and flushes that are virtually worthless. To underline this, anyone holding As, 10s, 8s, may calculate that they have a slightly better-than-even chance of completing the flush in a six-player game. But these odds only apply if all players stay to the showdown and no other spades appear amid their up cards, a scenario that is unrealistic even in the least competitive of games.

Right: A player takes a look at his hole card to confirm possession of three kings now that the final card has been dealt. Securing three of a kind in five cards will happen, on average, around once in every 35 deals. As in this instance, however, a player may have to wait until the final card to make the hand, so three possibly costly betting rounds will have already been negotiated.

PLAYABLE HANDS

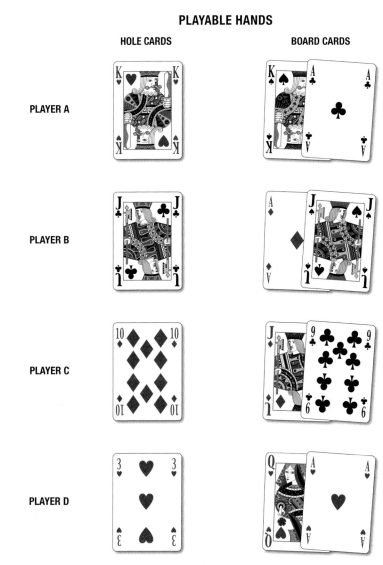

HOLE CARDS   **BOARD CARDS**

PLAYER A

PLAYER B

PLAYER C

PLAYER D

Above: Knowing which hands to play and which to fold on third street is crucial. A player with a pair of kings with an A kicker (the highest unpaired side card) is in a strong position. If no open pairs are visible, this hand will open the betting on third street. Similarly, having an A to support a hidden pair of jacks will intimidate opponents showing a K or a Q. Even if they have a hidden pair, the A will make them wary of calling a bet. Players holding three-card straights and flushes should fold on third street if an opponent bets as the chance of completing the hand is remote.

Effective strategies

The fact that most guidance on how to play five-card stud tends to advocate caution highlights how difficult it is, in limit poker particularly, to manipulate the betting and win large pots. On many occasions, the strength of a player's hand will be clearly apparent from the board cards, making it unlikely that an opponent will call a serious bet. Anyone with an open pair may double the minimum bet on third street in order to protect the hand, but this has two likely outcomes. Opponents with little chance of overtaking the hand will fold, while anyone who calls, let alone raises, is probably already ahead. Even if an opponent with just one up card higher than the open pair bets in the second round, then it is best to assume they have it beaten.

Pairing a mid-ranking hole card is not much better in this situation. For instance, a player who has paired a 9 in the hole with a card dealt face up will feel similarly vulnerable when there are several higher-ranking cards on the board. Any bet from an opponent showing A, Q, for example, will suggest that a third 9 is required to win. In a six-player game, a player will have seen a maximum of 13 cards – their three plus the ten other up cards, assuming everyone is still competing. Provided no other nines have appeared as yet, the chance of making trip nines in the next two rounds is never better than 8 to 1. Added to the fact that an opponent's hand might also improve, most players will fold rather than call in this situation, thus removing the temptation to commit further chips in the later rounds when the minimum bets increase.

Right: Player A cautiously calls the opening bet from player E, because, with two aces on the board already, the chances of either player C or E holding a pair are reduced. The fact that players C and D also decide to call rather than raise means neither has a pair as yet.

THE DEAL

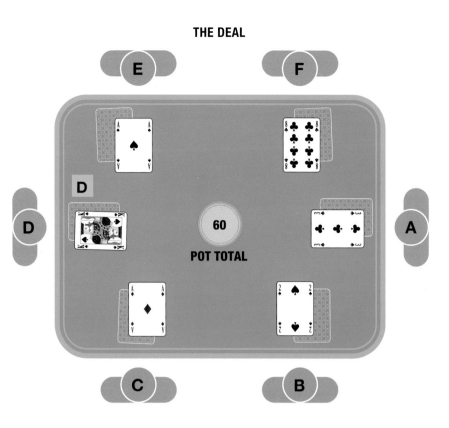

PLAYER A
Hole card

Above: In this 25/50 fixed-limit game, player A is dealt a pair of threes, which is useful, but no more than that, at present, given the high cards on the table. However, since it is 16 to 1 against any player being dealt a pair in the first two cards, there is a good chance that the pair of threes is currently leading.

OPENING BETTING ROUND

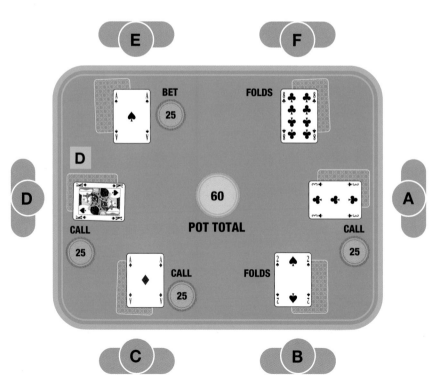

Bluffing

Opportunities to bluff in five-card stud do not arise very often in a fixed-limit game, since the cost of calling a bet is rarely prohibitive enough to force all opponents to fold. For a true bluff to be successful, each opponent must relinquish their claim on the pot. In games that involve ten players, there are usually enough cards in circulation to make bluffing with a weak hand on third street a risky proposition, in any case. Any player who has a reputation for tight play might capitalize on this image to perpetrate the occasional bluff, but then all experienced five-card stud players have a tendency to be extremely conservative in their approach. When playing against such opponents, a bluff on third street might be all that is needed to steal a small pot, but this is a manoeuvre best reserved for games with five or fewer players. Those players who wish to promote more bluffing in five-card stud are usually advised to play it as a pot-limit or no-limit game. The larger bets that are allowed have greater potential to intimidate opponents, which makes bluffing a much more viable prospect.

THIRD STREET

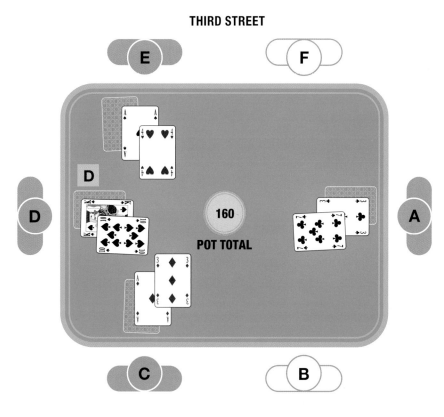

Above: The third card for each player brings no open pairs, but player A's chances of being dealt another 3 are compromised when the 3d is dealt to player C, there now being just one remaining unseen. If, as suspected, players C and E do not have pocket aces, then they may be reluctant to call a bet. But player D still has two overcards – cards higher than player A's threes – and probably represents the biggest danger given the possibility that he has a pocket K or 10 for a higher pair.

Right: Executing a bluff in five-card stud is more likely to succeed when the game is played with no-limit or pot-limit betting. As larger bets are permitted, opponents can be intimidated into folding with a hand such as this one.

> ### TIMING A BLUFF
> ♦ ♣ ♥ ♠
>
> Bluffing is more prevalent in pot-limit and no-limit games because of the greater freedom for players to make large bets. This increases the risk of sacrificing more chips on bluffs that fail, so a player needs to time the move correctly in order to lend any bluff credibility. For example if the opener shows an A after the deal, but is raised by a player whose door card is a lowly 6, then the bet suggests a pair is held. If the raise is big enough, it might take the pot uncontested, but, if not, any improvement in the hand – ideally another 6 – will reinforce the bluff and could persuade anyone holding a high pair to fold in the face of another large bet. Should one or other of the remaining sixes later be dealt to an opponent, the integrity of the bluff may quickly unravel. Players should therefore pay attention to the up cards at each stage, to determine whether the hand they are trying to represent has been compromised by events.

Fourth street

A typical game between six or more reasonable players is likely to feature a maximum of three or four contesting fourth street, and will probably only see a couple continue to the final round. Whichever betting structure is in operation, patience and due caution remain the recommended characteristics to exhibit during play. Players with poor chances of winning usually fold prior to fourth street, when the minimum bet routinely doubles for the remaining two betting rounds. Those who continue in the game can therefore be assumed to have the leading hand or one that has a fair chance of improving to be the best. Each remaining player will have three up cards showing at this stage, which makes an assessment of their ultimate hand's value quite simple

In terms of strategy, any player who is clearly ahead should capitalize on the situation by betting. Should everyone else fold, the player can take the pot, but any opponents who call, evidently do so in the belief that one or more cards in the deck may yet help them win. Offering the chance of a free card by checking in this situation represents poor play no matter how remote the opposition's chances of winning.

At the other end of the spectrum, a player with a trailing hand must realistically compare the pot odds with the odds against drawing a winning card. If the risk is unjustified, as is often the case, a player should fold in response to any bet, remembering that the bettor's hand may also improve. Players who harbour any doubts at all about the merit of their hand after four cards should check, when possible, whether first to act or not. Adopting a cautious approach such as this does, however, present the chance for players acting in late position to try stealing the occasional pot with a bluff.

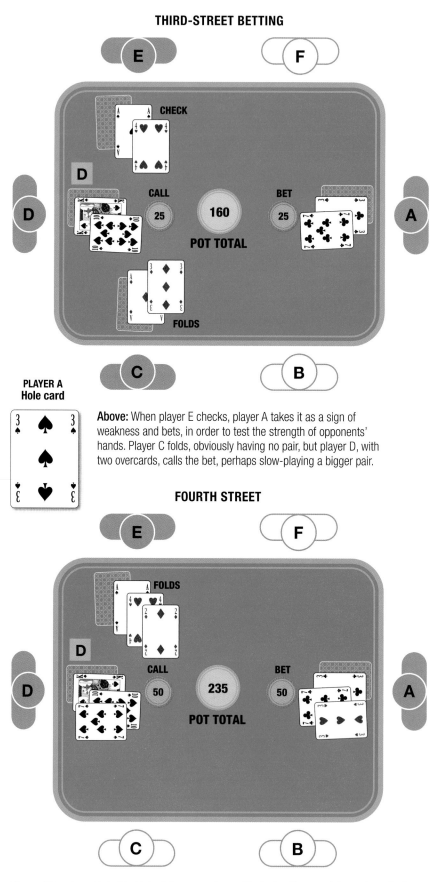

THIRD-STREET BETTING

PLAYER A
Hole card

Above: When player E checks, player A takes it as a sign of weakness and bets, in order to test the strength of opponents' hands. Player C folds, obviously having no pair, but player D, with two overcards, calls the bet, perhaps slow-playing a bigger pair.

FOURTH STREET

Above: After player E decided to call the second-round bets, fourth street brings player A trip (three) threes and the option to bet first with a pair of threes showing. Knowing the hand is definitely leading, player A rightly bets, forcing those who may have a winning opportunity to pay for their final card. Player D may make higher trips if holding a pair, but has given no indication yet that a K or 10 is held. It might be assumed that player D's hole card is another high-ranking spade. Player E folds, having no pair and, as player A now knows, no chance of a straight.

Reading the cards

Accurately reading the cards is crucial when forming any betting strategy on fourth street. By recalling the up cards previously folded and turned face down during play, as well as the various bets made by opponents in preceding rounds, a player has all the information needed to gauge the actual and potential strength of opposing hands. A player showing Ac, Jd, 9h, for instance, could have a pair of aces, with the possibility of making three of a kind if another A comes on fifth street. But if an A has already appeared among up cards that were folded earlier, the chances of the player fulfilling that potential are obviously reduced. Also, any opponent who does hold a pocket A will know for certain that, with only one remaining A unaccounted for, the player cannot have more than a pair of aces at present. If that is the case, then two pairs are the best the player can achieve, should a J or 9 appear on fifth street. If not, then the best possible hand the player showing Ac, Jd, 9h can hit is three jacks, assuming that the Jd is the only one of that rank to have appeared during the game. Deductive reasoning of this nature should guide betting decisions at this stage of play.

Fifth street

Once the final card has been dealt, there is little mystery concerning the competing hands, since, with only the hole cards obscured from view, their potential value can be quickly estimated. Typically, it is rare for more than two players to reach fifth street, which reduces final-round strategy to a couple of simple rules. A player who has possession of the winning hand should always bet at the first opportunity, in the hope that an opponent will call or even raise, thus boosting the size of the pot. By checking in this situation, a

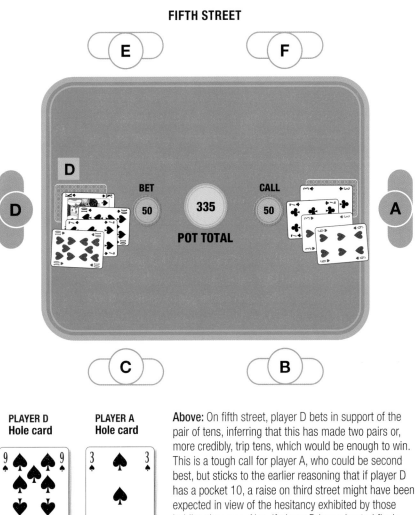

FIFTH STREET

PLAYER D
Hole card

PLAYER A
Hole card

Above: On fifth street, player D bets in support of the pair of tens, inferring that this has made two pairs or, more credibly, trip tens, which would be enough to win. This is a tough call for player A, who could be second best, but sticks to the earlier reasoning that if player D has a pocket 10, a raise on third street might have been expected in view of the hesitancy exhibited by those holding the aces. Also, if player D has a busted flush, then only a bluff can secure the pot. Player A therefore calls and wins with trip threes as player D's bluff, the hole being a 9s, is revealed.

player invites opponents to check, too, and so runs the risk of missing out on additional chips. Should a player be unsure of holding the winning hand, then a check is the best policy. Whether first to act or not, a bet may prompt an opponent to raise, at which point the player either forfeits the additional chips unnecessarily put into the pot or calls, uncomfortably, with what is probably a beaten hand.

Left: A player considers his next move at the table although, in five-card stud, the strategy to be adopted on fifth street is usually straightforward. If it is evident from the board cards that an opponent possesses a weaker hand, a player should bet and hope for a call.

SEVEN-CARD STUD

Seven-card stud starts with each player contributing an ante to the pot prior to the deal. Cards are then dealt one at a time until everyone has three cards, two face down, variously described as hidden, pocket or hole cards, and one face up, known as the door card. The player with the lowest door card opens the betting, typically by making a compulsory bet for a sum less than the usual minimum bet permitted. After the first round, those still in the game each receive a fourth card, face up, prior to the next round of betting. From this point, the first player to act is the one now showing the best visible hand. In this (the second) and subsequent rounds there is no obligation to bet and players may check. Players receive a fifth and sixth card face up, and a seventh card face down with the deal of each punctuated by additional rounds of betting. Players still in the game at the showdown have seven cards from which to make a five-card poker hand, four face up and three face down. The winner is the player who either makes an uncalled bet or who displays the best five-card poker hand once the fifth and final betting round has concluded.

The game of seven-card stud developed from the five-card variation and became popular during the years leading up to World War II. Having travelled the world with the US military, seven-card stud emerged afterwards as the most widely played form of poker and dominated the commercial scene in both Las Vegas and Europe for nearly 40 years. Indeed, up until the 1980s a couple of the more famous Las Vegas casinos offered only seven-card stud in their poker rooms.

Though challenged by Texas Hold 'em for contemporary favouritism, seven-card stud remains a very challenging game which draws upon the whole gamut of any poker player's skills in order to prove rewarding. The five betting rounds help to generate sizeable pots, relative to the stake-levels in operation, and the exposed cards offer a great deal of information as a hand progresses. Yet the fact that players who sustain interest to the showdown will have three of their cards face down still leaves room for doubt in the minds of opposition over the composition of anyone's hand. This creates the opportunity for some imaginative play and leaves the way open for players to consider the occasional bluff, especially in the pot-limit version of

LIKELY WINNING HANDS

FIG 1: TWO PAIRS

| HOLE CARDS | UP CARDS | SEVENTH STREET |

FIG 2: THREE OF A KIND

| HOLE CARDS | UP CARDS | SEVENTH STREET |

Above: The quality of hand required to win at the showdown will be dictated by the nature of the game and the stakes for which players are competing. In high-stakes fixed-limit games, particularly those incorporating the use of substantial antes, players with good starting hands are prone to bet aggressively right away. Such games are therefore likely to see just two or three players involved at any showdown with hands such as two high pairs or three of a kind often proving good enough to win. Fig 1 features two pairs of aces and kings, a hand completed by the 9 kicker (the highest unpaired side card in that player's hand) which could prove decisive in the unlikely event that an opponent also has aces and kings. Fig 2 shows a hand comprising three jacks, the discounted cards in this case being the 3c and 4c.

Below: This picture highlights the fact that, in seven-card stud, a player must count five cards from the seven ultimately available in order to make a viable poker hand. Here, the 8h and 5d are redundant since the player will count the remaining five cards to make a full house of aces over kings.

COST OF INFORMATION

♦ ♣ ♥ ♠

Before the cards are dealt, it must be understood that the level of the antes and bring-in bets may vary from one poker room to another, irrespective of betting limits. Games featuring low antes tend to encourage loose play and can provide rich pickings for a tight, conservative player who is prepared to wait for a strong hand before committing chips to the pot. Players who enjoy being regularly involved in the action should probably play with higher antes as this helps to inflate the pot and capitalize on their good hands, offsetting the losses which come from contesting a high proportion of pots. Many guides to seven-card stud focus on high-stakes games in which tight but aggressive play is the norm. In these, players who are not disciplined enough to fold opening hands may be drawn into situations where their hands improve but still trail that of the aggressor who has two aims in mind. The first is to reduce the field to maybe one opponent, the second is to ensure that players with inferior starting hands pay the maximum amount for the chance to improve. When playing such opponents, calling for a couple of rounds in the expectation of help from the deck can soon reduce a player's chip stack. In social games, the betting is quite restrained with players often content to wait until fifth street before deciding whether to play or fold. The key factor in both types of game is that the betting levels rise on fifth street for the final three rounds, when any player who wants to see extra cards will inevitably pay more for the privilege.

the game. However, this betting structure is most popular among experienced players and those who prefer low-stakes, social poker are more inclined to play fixed- or spread-limit stud.

Early considerations

At the beginning of the game, every player is dealt three cards, the first two are face down and the third – the door card – face up. In common with all poker variations, the decision on which of these opening hands might be worth playing should be determined by an understanding of what is likely to prove to be a winning hand at the showdown. This, in turn, is affected by the culture of the game and whether it is a volatile, low-stakes contest, between loose players, or a tight game between experienced players.

Ordinarily, at least two pairs, probably including aces, will be required to claim victory and three of a kind is often good enough. However, if the cost of betting is not too restrictive, then the likelihood of players chasing straights or better is much greater and could render the average winning hand of two pairs extremely vulnerable. In a low-stakes game, even a player in possession of three eights by fourth street, for example, may not be able to bet a sufficiently large amount to dissuade opponents from calling with inferior hands that still hold the potential for substantial improvement. It is therefore worth remembering that when four or five players stay to see a fifth card, the rank of the winning hand will quite often be higher than two pairs or three of a kind.

Below: A restrained low-stakes game which features little in the way of forceful betting prior to fifth street could easily see several players willing to continue to the showdown. When the betting is light, more players remain involved and initially unpromising hands are given the chance to develop into winners. Strong hands such as straights, flushes and full houses are more likely to occur, although sometimes a solitary pair will still win.

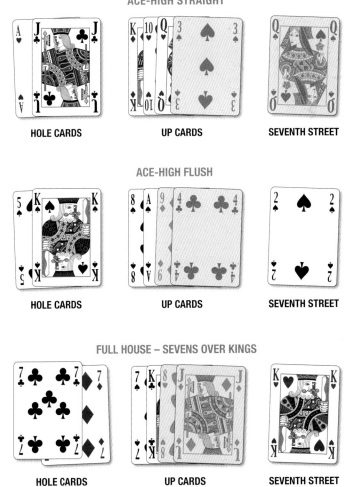

BETTER THAN AVERAGE HANDS

ACE-HIGH STRAIGHT

| HOLE CARDS | UP CARDS | SEVENTH STREET |

ACE-HIGH FLUSH

| HOLE CARDS | UP CARDS | SEVENTH STREET |

FULL HOUSE – SEVENS OVER KINGS

| HOLE CARDS | UP CARDS | SEVENTH STREET |

Starting hands

Assessing the value of the first three cards received will very much depend on the style of game. In a tight game, featuring first-round raises and plenty of folding, only the very best starting hands may warrant support, although this may reduce a player's participation to around one in five hands on average. Social games are likely to feature much more leeway regarding which hands to play, but this does not disguise the fact that it is advantageous to start with any one of five key combinations.

The best possible starting hand is three of a kind, or trips, with high pairs of aces, kings or queens are also highly prized. A starting hand featuring a low pocket pair and a high-value door card (the player's first exposed or 'up' card) such as an A or K may also be worth playing as are three-card flushes and open-ended three-card straights.

Being dealt these combinations does not guarantee victory and players must observe the up cards held by opponents as the game unfolds. This is why players bet aggressively with strong hands when the antes are high in order to end the contest quickly and rake in the chips, winning these small pots being crucial to keeping the cost of the antes at bay.

Rolled-up trips

There are 22,100 possible three-card combinations available from the standard 52-card deck and the best of these, naturally, is trip aces which will materialize only once in every 5,525 deals on average. Although such a hand is very powerful, the fact is that any three of a kind may well win even without improvement, and the probability of being dealt 'rolled-up trips' – three of a kind in the first three cards – is rated at 424 to 1. The great benefit of seeing such a hand is that its strength is hidden during the early part of the game,

ROLLED-UP TRIPS

HOLE CARDS   HOLE CARDS   HOLE CARDS

DOOR CARD   DOOR CARD   DOOR CARD

Above: Being dealt any three of a kind presents a player with a huge advantage since the hand will often be enough to win on its own while also having an excellent chance of improving to a full house. But the odds against receiving any three of a kind in the first three cards are 424 to 1, while finding a pair of aces in the hole to match the door card for trip aces will happen about once in every 5,525 deals. When a player holds such a starting hand, a winning outcome should be expected with the main concern being to manage the pot for the maximum possible gain.

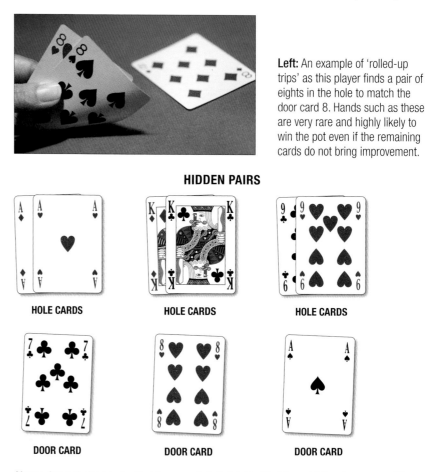

Left: An example of 'rolled-up trips' as this player finds a pair of eights in the hole to match the door card 8. Hands such as these are very rare and highly likely to win the pot even if the remaining cards do not bring improvement.

HIDDEN PAIRS

HOLE CARDS   HOLE CARDS   HOLE CARDS

DOOR CARD   DOOR CARD   DOOR CARD

Above: Any pair dealt in the first three cards is helpful but holding a high pair – aces or kings – will give a player an early advantage. Having the pair concealed enhances that advantage as it allows a player to bet in a fashion that disguises the strength of the hand. Someone holding pocket aces and showing a 7 can justifiably call any first-round bet or raise by an opponent and should certainly make the first raise if acting from an early betting position. Opponents may suspect the hand is better than a pair of sevens but they will be wary of other possibilities.

although playing low trips can be problematic. A player in possession of three threes may well bring in the betting and find that a couple of opponents showing a K and an A respectively both put in a raise. Since they have to be credited with at least a high pair each, a further raise with just a 3 showing will alert them to danger and even a call will put them on their guard.

In most cases, professionals advocate supporting a strong opening hand with maximum bets since underplaying it to keep opponents involved can backfire. However, on rare occasions when rolled-up trips materialize, players can usually afford to bet the minimum and keep opponents involved in the action until the time is right to strike with a large bet. Although opposition hands may improve sufficiently to threaten the early advantage obtained from holding trips, the odds against this hand itself improving to a full house with four cards still to come are only just over two to one. Given that it may also improve to something higher than a full house, it is almost certain that a player dealt trips in the first three cards is going to play to the showdown unless there is strong evidence to suggest an opponent has a higher-ranking full house or better.

SPLIT PAIRS

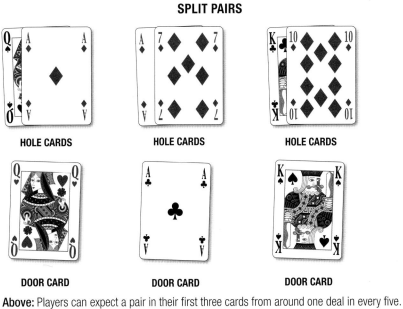

| HOLE CARDS | HOLE CARDS | HOLE CARDS |
| DOOR CARD | DOOR CARD | DOOR CARD |

Above: Players can expect a pair in their first three cards from around one deal in every five. On many occasions this will feature the door card matching a hole card for a 'split pair' which, although beneficial in the case of high pairs, makes disguising the hand difficult. Ordinarily, any first-round bet from a player showing an A, K or Q will be interpreted as representing a pair, allowing scope for a bluff when a player holds just a high card and no pair. By contrast, a player who does hold a split pair of aces but simply calls the bring-in from an early betting position may lull opponents into sensing weakness. Should one of them raise the betting, a subsequent call or re-raise from the player holding the door card A will dispel that notion immediately.

Right: Another decent starting hand in the shape of a split pair, a K in the hole being matched with a door-card K. If no other kings are showing amid opponents' door cards and aces are also absent from the board, a solid bet in the first round is certainly justifiable.

Pairs
♦ ♣ ♥ ♠

The chances of being dealt a pair among the first three cards in seven-card stud are fractionally less than 5 to 1, although it is around 25 to 1 against receiving jacks or better. While they offer potential for improvement, players must weigh up the merits of holding a hidden pair or a split pair, the former meaning that both paired cards are dealt face down while a split pair, as the name suggests, is one in which the door card matches a hole card. Obviously, it is easier to play deceptively when holding pocket aces and showing a 7 than it is if one of the aces is a door card. Opponents will expect a bet in support of the A on display and will be wary of becoming too involved given the potential for it to be paired with a hole card. In this situation, it can be assumed that any opponents who do call to see fourth street are holding reasonable hands. Nevertheless, they could only be leading a pair of aces and a 7 kicker, in this instance, if holding three of a kind or the other pair of aces with a higher-ranking odd card. A maximum bet when the aces are hidden and the 7 is showing might flush out those opponents holding decent hands without them having a clear idea of the strength truly represented by the first-round bet.

Three-card straights

Open-ended three-card straights, such as 7, 8, 9 or J, Q, K, offer attractive potential as starting hands as the chances of converting them into a full straight are around 6 to 1. Players can expect to see three cards to a straight regularly, maybe as often as one in six deals, making them appealing hands to play in a restrained betting game which regularly features four or five players paying for a fifth card.

In an eight-handed game, each player can see ten cards following the deal, these being their own three cards and the seven door cards in front of their opponents. If holding the 7, 8, 9 combination, for example, any 5, 6, 10 or J on fourth street immediately increases a player's chances of making the straight. Improvement is also ensured if a 7, 8 or 9 is dealt to make a pair which means that up to 25 cards in the deck have the potential to help the hand. However, several of those cards could already be visible on the table and this is the key factor in deciding how far to proceed in a bid to complete the straight. If an opponent with a 10 showing chooses to raise the betting, it would be realistic to assume at least a pair of tens is being

THREE-CARD STRAIGHTS

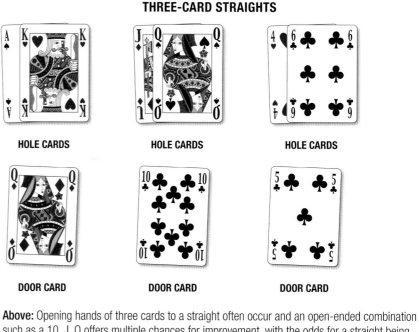

HOLE CARDS   HOLE CARDS   HOLE CARDS

DOOR CARD   DOOR CARD   DOOR CARD

Above: Opening hands of three cards to a straight often occur and an open-ended combination such as a 10, J, Q offers multiple chances for improvement, with the odds for a straight being completed after seven cards of around 6 to 1. Higher-ranking three-card combinations of 10 and above offer the potential for an A-high straight. Pairing any of these with subsequent cards could allow a player to take the pot before a showdown. This is less likely when a player holds low-ranking cards such as 4, 5, 6 and makes one or even two low pairs. But, should a straight come by fifth street, perhaps with a 7 and a 3, the hand may still be a poor betting option if an opponent seems to be drawing to a higher-ranking straight or a flush. If fourth and fifth street bring no improvement to a hand such as this, it is probably best to fold at the first large bet.

Left: Three suited picture cards such as the K, Q, J are generally worth support, especially if the game features little in the way of aggressive betting in the early rounds. The combination is such that half the remaining cards in the deck offer the potential to improve the hand. This is usually enough of an incentive to bet for at least a couple of rounds.

LOW PAIRS, BIG KICKERS
♦ ♣ ♥ ♠

Though they can be more dangerous to play, medium or low pocket pairs still have the same potential for improvement as pairs of aces or kings. The problem is that a player holding the low pair must improve when up against such cards, a prospect made easier if the kicker (the highest-value unpaired card in their hand) is of a high rank. For example an opening bet from an opponent showing a K, and so probably representing a pair, is worth calling if a player holds pocket tens with an A kicker. Such a call implies possession of a reasonable hand, possibly a pair of aces, and could enable the player to see another card or two quite cheaply against the probable pair of kings. Should an A materialize on fourth street to provide an open pair, the player will act first while the opponent holding kings ponders whether any bet indicates trip aces, and not just the pair on display. If a 10 is dealt instead, then a well-disguised three of a kind is secured along with an opportunity to dominate the betting, provided the opponent has not been dealt another K. As with the three-card flush and straight examples, deciding whether to support an opening hand with a small pair is generally based on the possibility of catching a good card on fourth street. If this fails to happen and opponents' hands clearly improve, it is wiser to fold than to continue betting. This helps to avoid the disastrous possibility of improving sufficiently to play to the showdown with what remains the second-best hand.

represented. Immediately, this reduces the prospects of making anything better than a 9-high straight since half the tens in the deck could already be out. On top of that, even pairing a 7, 8 or 9 on fourth street will still leave the player trailing and would make further participation in the hand inadvisable.

Three-card flushes

Flushes outrank straights and the chances of being dealt three assorted cards of the same suit are correspondingly longer at around 24 to 1. Though a flush is a likely winner, disguising a flush draw can be more difficult with each round making it vital that, in pursuing the hand, a player is well aware how many cards of the relevant suit are already in play.

A player holding Kh, 10h, 6h, for instance, has a 5 to 1 chance of making the flush, an appealing prospect after the deal though these odds assume no knowledge of the opposition's cards. If there are hearts among the door cards on the table, then the odds against completing the hand obviously lengthen. As with the straight draw, there are four rounds in which to hit the two hearts that will make the hand but, if missing them on fourth and fifth street, the rising cost of trying to catch them could become prohibitive. For this reason, though three-card flushes have a fair chance of developing into winning hands, they are rarely worth pursuing beyond fourth street in the face of aggressive betting from an opponent.

Drawing hands such as flushes and straights are generally played cautiously, with solid players recognizing that support should be confined to those comprising high-ranking cards only. These provide insurance since pairing aces, kings or queens when drawing to flushes and straights can offer another route to victory should the initial promise of the hand not be realized.

THREE-CARD FLUSHES

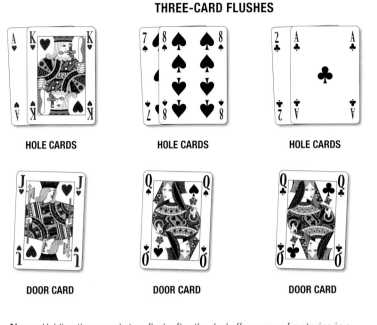

HOLE CARDS HOLE CARDS HOLE CARDS

DOOR CARD DOOR CARD DOOR CARD

Above: Holding three cards to a flush after the deal offers scope for staying in a hand, though a player will hope to draw the cards needed to complete the flush cheaply. Calling an opponent's first-round raise is justified if a player holds an A, but help must materialize quickly in the face of aggressive betting to warrant further participation. If two or more cards of the relevant suit are among the opposition's door cards, any attempt to pursue the flush draw should be entertained with caution. High cards are of more value because they present alternative chances to win if the flush draw is derailed.

LOW PAIRS WITH BIG KICKER

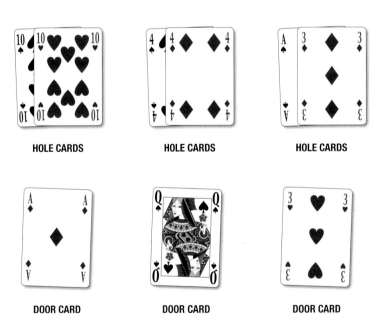

HOLE CARDS HOLE CARDS HOLE CARDS

DOOR CARD DOOR CARD DOOR CARD

Above: Though not without potential, starting hands that feature both hidden and split low pairs are immediately vulnerable and will usually need a helpful card on fourth street to encourage a player to continue in all but the lightest of betting heats. To this end, having a high-ranking kicker – ideally an A – to supplement the pair is preferable since pairing the kicker for two pairs could transform a modest hand into a likely winner. For example should a player with a split pair of threes and an A in the hole catch another A on fourth street, the hand could already be strong enough to win while its true value can be disguised if betting remains light. Slow-playing the hand is possible though a raise should be considered if any open pairs lower than aces are visible after four cards.

Third-street strategy

A common mistake players frequently make is to overestimate the value of their starting hands, following which they bet modestly to keep several opponents involved in the game to help swell the pot. There are so many possibilities at work in seven-card stud that opponents with the weakest of hands can improve past, for example, a high-value opening pair. Consequently, players who are dealt a premium hand of a high pair, and possibly even three high cards offering powerful straight and flush potential, should bet aggressively in the opening round to advertise strength and encourage opponents to fold. The exception to this is when a player holds trips since the time to exert pressure in this case is on fifth street, when the betting levels rise and opponents with drawing hands may feel they are committed to the pot. For example a player who is dealt three nines when there are two or three higher up cards visible should sit tight and just call any opening-round bets whenever possible. Raising in the opening round may be justified from a late betting position if opponents possessing higher door cards – their first exposed or 'up' cards – have so far been content to call. They may think the raise represents an attempt to steal the pot with a pair of nines, in which case their higher-ranking up cards could tempt them into staying for another round or two. However, if an opponent showing an A, for example, has already raised the betting, a re-raise will be read as confirmation of trip nines. This may be enough to take the pot, but calling the raise is a better option in this situation since the meaning behind the bet is more difficult to interpret. By generating an element of doubt in the minds of opponents, the player is more likely to maximize the profit on a probable winning hand.

THE DEAL

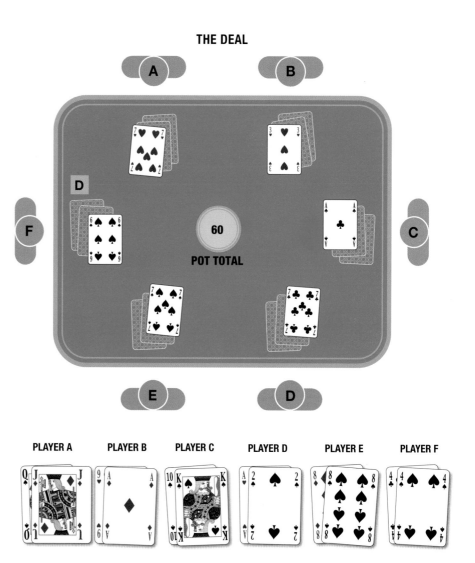

| PLAYER A | PLAYER B | PLAYER C | PLAYER D | PLAYER E | PLAYER F |

Above: The scene following the deal in a 50/100 fixed-limit seven-card stud game, with the pot already comprising an ante of 10 chips from each player. Player E's pocket eights is the best hand at present while player F also has a pair in the hole, although the fours are clearly weak. Player C, with high-ranking cards to support the A on display, is in a good position to pressurize opponents given the lack of any door cards higher than his 10 in the hole.

ALL-IN

One of the key elements of table-stakes poker is that players can never be priced out of a hand when they have insufficient chips to call an opponent's bet. In this situation, players may push all their chips into the pot and declare that they are 'all-in' or, if preferred, 'tapped-out'. Should they hold the winning hand at the showdown, they may only claim from their opponents a sum equal to that which they have staked. So a player calling all-in for 100 chips when the bet is 200 may only claim 100 chips from each of those who made the full bet. The rest of the chips constitute a side pot that is contested by the other players. In no-limit poker, the all-in bet can be a powerful tactical ploy, since players are permitted, at their turn, to bet all their chips at any stage of the game.

Door cards

Assessing the potential of any three-card starting hand is the most crucial factor in deciding whether to take part after the deal. To this end, knowing which hands are likely to secure an early advantage is important, but there are, as always, other factors to bear in mind. The most obvious source of these comes in the value of the opponents' door cards since these must always have an influence on any player's strategy.

Holding a concealed pair of aces with a J as the door card is a good opening hand, but its potential for improvement would obviously be compromised if the two remaining aces in the deck were visible among the opposition's up cards. Possession of the top pair at the outset normally confers an advantage and offers a player the chance to bet aggressively to reduce the competition. The danger in not doing so is that more picture cards will be dealt to opponents in subsequent rounds, perhaps creating an open pair or two, at which point a reassessment of the strength of the pair of aces will be needed. By fifth street, it may be clear that two pairs will not be enough to win and that the chances of catching the K, Q and 10 needed for a straight have all but evaporated.

Again, it is worth stressing that players must keep a watchful eye on the up cards as they are dealt, remember any that have been folded, and constantly re-calculate the changing value of the cards in their possession.

DISGUISING A HAND
♦ ♣ ♥ ♠

One of the better drawing hands to be dealt is a three-card flush which features a low-ranking door card with two higher cards in the hole, particularly when one of those is the A. Pairing the A in this instance could be the springboard for further investment in the hand since it gives insurance against the flush itself not materializing by offering another chance to secure the pot. If there are any cards of the relevant suit already on the board then the flush draw becomes less likely, but the potential for disguising the merit of the hand is high when no other cards of that suit are visible. For instance, with the Ac, Kc in the hole and the 8c as a door card, calling a raise in the opening round from an opponent showing a lower door card than an A or K gives away few clues regarding the hand held, most opponents being likely to credit the player with a pair of eights at best. Indeed, a re-raise at this point could have opponents thinking that a high pocket pair is held, rather than two other clubs, such that another club on fourth street could seem quite innocuous.

Should this happen, the chances of converting the four-card flush into a five-card hand are about even money which will normally be enough to persuade a player to stay to the showdown, provided the flush still appears to be a probable winner.

FIRST-ROUND BETTING

Right: Player B makes the compulsory – or forced – bet known as the bring-in by virtue of holding the lowest door card. To offset this obligation, the bring-in is set at 25 chips, not 50. Player C immediately 'completes the bet' by betting 50 chips and raising the level to the accepted minimum for the first two betting rounds. Player D folds because with one A and two sevens already in play, his own hand of A, 2, 7 is rendered worthless. The remainder all call, including player B who contributes the additional 25 chips to make up the betting.

Fourth street

The arrival of fourth street sees another card dealt face up to those players still in the game while the opening bet in this round, and all subsequent rounds, is the preserve of the player showing the best hand. Importantly, the player in this position is not obliged to bet and may check if desired, a privilege not extended to the holder of the low card in the previous betting round.

In terms of strategy, how to respond to events after the fourth card is dealt depends on the nature of the game. Tight but aggressive opponents assumedly have a promising hand and if fourth street brings them obvious mprovement, they are likely to press home the advantage with a bet or, when in late position, a raise. Defending against such strong play in a serious-money game is only advised with a hand that is either already powerful or, as in the case of a flush draw, has multiple opportunities to become a winner with any one of several cards.

In a similar vein, although more liberties are taken by players in low-stakes games regarding which hands to play as far as fifth street, they must still consider their chances of making a better-than-average hand. Since more players are

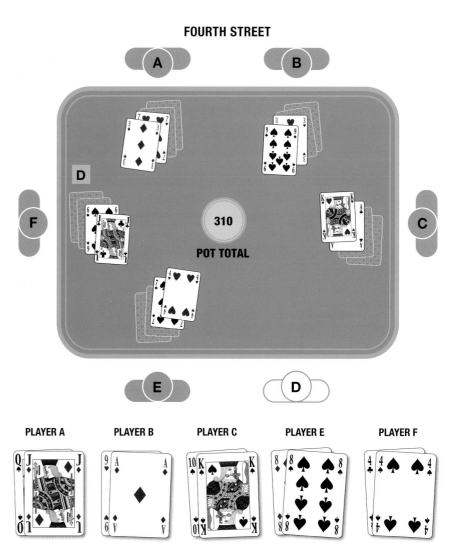

FOURTH STREET

| PLAYER A | PLAYER B | PLAYER C | PLAYER E | PLAYER F |

Above: Fourth street brings help in the shape of a pair for both players B and C and, with no pair on the board at present, they may feel this has given them an advantage. In player C's case, the K provides the top pair and a good opportunity to exert more pressure on opponents given the apparent lack of danger represented among the other cards visible on the table. For those holding the pocket pairs there may be just enough incentive to see a fifth card, but player A is definitely in trouble.

Right: Holding a hand such as this open-ended straight-flush draw on fourth street will tempt most players to continue betting given that any club will make a flush while any 9 or 4 will complete a straight, and possibly even a straight flush. These all have the potential to emerge as winning hands at the showdown.

likely to continue to the showdown, when players remaining in the hand reveal their cards to determine the winner, the opportunity for back-door straights and flushes to develop increases, meaning that even two pairs will not be good enough on many occasions.

Premium hands

Identifying the most promising hands on fourth street logically follows the same criteria as that applied after the deal. Anyone holding three of a kind – trips – of whatever rank is in a strong position, although this may be weakened from a betting perspective if an open pair on fourth street matches a player's hole card. A player with an open pair of kings who raised the betting in the previous round, for example, will alert the opposition to the likely presence of trip kings, a very powerful hand. An opening bet is likely to win the pot immediately, thus reducing the profitability of the hand, while exercising the option to check will typically result in everyone else checking since they will, quite rightly, suspect a trap is being set. Though trip kings is still likely to be the leading hand after five cards and will usually go on to win, this tactic does offer a chance for opponents to improve at no cost, which rarely constitutes good poker.

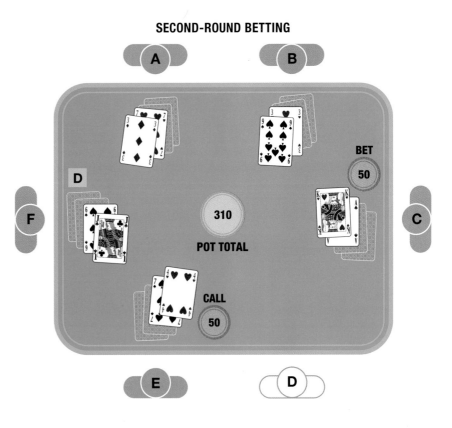

SECOND-ROUND BETTING

310
POT TOTAL

BET 50

CALL 50

Above: Player C duly opens the betting and is called by player E who has the pair of eights and is hoping to find some help on fifth street for the minimum cost. However, with several cards that may complete a low-ranking straight already in play, this is a questionable decision. Realistically, only an 8 for three of a kind will instil any confidence in player E's hand.

Holding any two pairs on fourth street is another good position to be in although, once again, it is better to have two up cards of different rank matching the two in the hole. This conceals the strength of the hand while having an open pair combined with a hidden pair is evidently much more revealing. Other hands that almost demand to be played are high-ranking four-card flushes and open-ended straights, along with three-card flushes and straights that are supplemented by a high pair.

Controlled Aggression
♦ ♣ ♥ ♠

When holding well-disguised high-ranking trips on fourth street, or two high pairs including aces, the key to maximizing the advantage comes from keeping opponents involved in the pot. Because the strength of the hand is concealed, a player can normally afford to check the betting and offer a free card, or make a minimum bet to induce others to call. Controlling the urge to raise on fourth street paves the way for more aggressive betting in the later rounds when the stakes rise. One or two opponents may have improved sufficiently by then to feel committed to the pot with drawing hands that would still not be good enough to win even if completed. By contrast, players who hold low-ranking trips or two pairs usually cannot afford to exercise such restraint on fourth street and are generally advised to bet or raise the maximum when the chance comes. In this situation, the objective is to force opponents with drawing hands to fold, particularly those with high-ranking but, as yet, unpaired door cards.

Strategic ploys

For the most part, the strategies applied in the opening betting rounds of a seven-card stud game are similar to those in other poker variations. Players who believe they have the lead should bet accordingly and force opponents to pay more for a chance to take the pot.

The exception to this policy comes when a player holds a distinctly powerful hand that is likely to win without progress. Chances such as this do not arise very often, so players need to exercise a degree of flexibility when betting on fourth street. This is unavoidable since the number of cards in play and the permutations that result prevent any dogmatic approach to the game beyond this stage.

Most guides to seven-card stud highlight a range of hands that, by fourth street, have the potential to become winners. Apart from some of the examples already described, even a hand comprising three cards ranked 10 or higher, but with no pair, is sometimes worth playing. The decision on whether to do so, however, will be dictated by the betting patterns exhibited and the number of open cards already seen. Holding 4s, 10c, Jd, Kh, for example, can only be appealing if there are few cards of the same rank or higher in play. If an array of different picture cards is on display and the betting is heavy, then the value of the hand is considerably diminished since a flush is already impossible and a straight may be very unlikely. This highlights the importance of interpreting the information on offer at the table, rather than relying on a rigid concept of which hands to play.

Right: A hand such as this has limited potential to improve with two cards needed for a straight and a flush already impossible by virtue of holding a card in each suit. Only if the betting is very light and the opposition's face-up cards are of medium-to-low rank should a player persevere. If fifth street brings no help, ideally via a Q, then a decision to fold would be wise.

RAISING IN LATE POSITION

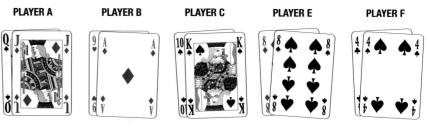

Above: As the second-round betting continues, player F also makes a poor decision by calling given that player E has been dealt a 4, one of the few cards that could immediately improve player F's hand. The pot continues to grow, however, making it difficult to resist taking a chance on another card. Player A's hand is folded but player B makes a raise in late position with the pair of nines. The suggestion that two pairs or possibly three nines have been secured is designed to test the character of the opposition.

PLAYER A	PLAYER B	PLAYER C	PLAYER E	PLAYER F

Stealing the pot

In low-stakes fixed-limit games, the chances of stealing the pot on fourth street with a raise are limited. It is usually not possible to bet a sufficient amount to force everyone else to fold. Pot-limit stud, however, offers players a little more leeway when making such a move. This is because a pot-sized bet is hard to call, even at this stage, for opponents holding marginal hands such as small pairs, or three-card flushes and straights. Trying a bluff along these lines is best when in a late betting position and the action has been checked around the table, inferring no one has great faith in their cards. If successful, it enables a player to cover the cost of the antes for several more rounds.

If the bluff is uncovered, this is far from disastrous as it shows a willingness to take a chance with a weak hand which may bring reward later. A bet in a similar situation when holding a strong hand is more likely to be called by opponents who have seen a player's tendency to bluff. Such hands have a greater chance of being paid off by opponents too suspicious to take the hint.

FREE CARDS
♦ ♣ ♥ ♠

Securing more cards as cheaply as possible is vital when holding a viable hand. One way to do this is to raise the betting on fourth street with a hand that is trailing but has potential. Assuming the bet is called but nobody has any obvious help on fifth street, the opposition could warily check the betting around and allow sixth street to be dealt for free. The extra bet on fourth street, which amounts to a semi-bluff, will have saved the player from making a bet at the increased level in the next round. The winning chance of the hand can then be re-assessed with just one more card to come and two further betting rounds to negotiate.

BUILDING THE POT

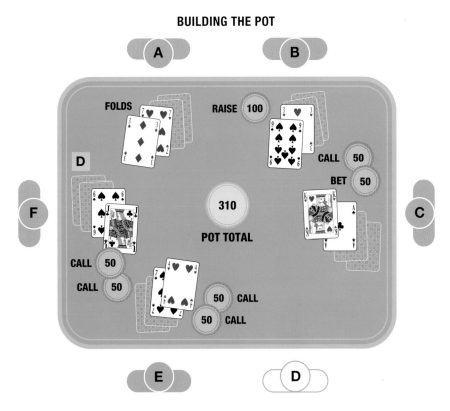

Above: Following player B's raise, player C could re-raise to try driving players E and F out of the pot but, respectful of the bet from player B, decides that the call is a better option. This allows players E and F to follow suit with a call, ensuring that the pot continues to grow and presenting the first player to act in the next round with immediate pot odds of a tempting 7 to 1.

Above: Player B pairs the pocket 9 on fourth street and, acting last, decides to raise given the lack of aggression exhibited in the second round of betting. Although three opponents call the raise, a move such as this is enough to keep them on their guard since they will be aware it could signify three nines are already held.

Fifth street

When playing seven-card stud there are two critical points at which a player must decide whether to participate in a hand, these being after the deal and then again on fifth street. Being able to distinguish a promising opening hand from a poor one is essential, but such promise usually needs to show signs of fulfilment by fifth street for a player to consider any further betting. Since the minimum bet doubles from the third round onwards, players still needing to draw cards for a probable winning hand can expect to pay dearly when trying to catch them. An experienced opponent with a leading hand will certainly ensure this is the case.

Assuming a player has a pair of aces and a four-card straight, holding Ac, Qc in the hole and Kc, Js, Ad on the board, the decision on whether to proceed or not will depend on the strength of hand it is possible to achieve and the likelihood of it occurring. If the four tens, several picture cards and a handful of clubs remain unseen, then the number of live cards available to improve the hand beyond a pair of aces makes participation on fifth street highly likely.

However, these possibilities will be of less interest should an opponent who raised in the opening round with a 7 showing now possess a board comprising trip sevens. If the remaining 7 is in play, a pocket pair is the obvious inference to be drawn from the original raise meaning that a full house must now be suspected. The player holding the pair of aces, expecting the straight and flush draws to be redundant, would need to draw live cards on sixth and seventh streets to improve, though the odds against hitting a full house are 39 to 1. Obtaining a royal flush or four of a kind under these circumstances is highly improbable even if the relevant cards have yet to appear on the table.

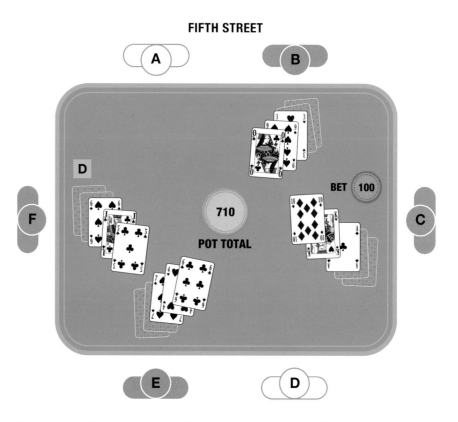

Above: Once the fifth card has been dealt, the betting levels rise making this the critical moment in the game. Anyone who bets at this point is likely to continue to the showdown, especially when a fixed-limit betting structure is in operation, as in this example. The size of the pot often becomes too big to resist if players can see they have a chance, however remote, of making the winning hand. Player C acts first once more here with the best hand showing – still the A-high – with the two high pairs of kings and tens well disguised.

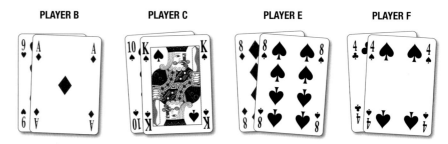

Below: On the face of it this appears to be an attractive hand on fifth street since the pair of aces is supplemented by high-ranking cards. Any 10 will complete a straight while pairing the K, Q or J for two high pairs might just prove enough. But whether to bet or not at this stage will very much depend on how many of these key cards have already been seen in play during the hand.

Promising positions

Although it is possible that a lowly pair of twos on fifth street could blossom into four of a kind by the time of the showdown, there are many more promising positions to be in at this point in the game. The general consensus among poker critics is that any hand of aces up or better has to be played, with disguised high pairs and trips remaining very strong hands. Players who have already completed straights will obviously expect to continue in the hand unless an opponent's up cards and betting suggest that a higher straight or a flush is likely to be held. Finding such a hand in five cards will normally guarantee the lead but it can still be difficult to fend off speculative opponents with drawing hands in a low-stakes, fixed-limit game.

The escalating size of the pot, relative to the cost of a bet, will often encourage opponents to call in the third round even though they know they are trailing. In pot-limit stud, by contrast, a player with a made straight can advertise the fact with a pot-sized raise, thus making it much more expensive to call for those opponents still needing additional cards to win.

Below: Any player holding two medium or low pairs on fifth street, like the eights and fours shown here, could be leading but remains vulnerable if unable to force opponents to fold. This is true in fixed-limit poker when the size of the permitted bet may not be intimidating enough to prevent several of them from calling.

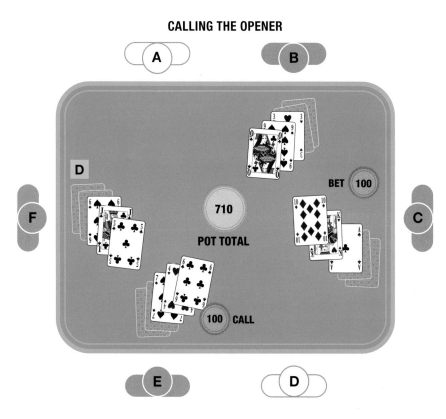

Above: The 6c presents player E with a small chance of hitting a straight although the 5 dealt to player F does not help. A raise now might be enough to suggest to opponents that the straight is already made but, with so many chips already in the pot, player E realizes that even a bet of 200 will be unlikely to dissuade them from calling. Consequently, player E simply calls for 100.

COMPROMISING SITUATIONS
♦ ♣ ♥ ♠

As might be expected, there is a wide variety of hands that can prove tempting for a player to support from fifth street onwards, the most dangerous being leading hands that are still likely to need improvement in order to prevail. A player holding two medium or low pairs, perhaps holding 9c, 8s, 4h, 8d, 4c, will not feel secure unless dealt another 8 or 4, the chances of which depend upon how many of those remaining are still live. Opponents with higher open pairs or who have previously represented possession of a concealed high pair, could easily have several cards in play that will win them the pot.

A solitary pair of aces is another hand that could frequently be leading after five cards, and most players will probably pursue it to the river – the seventh and final card dealt – if the board suggests no obvious threat. When up against four or five opponents, however, a high pair will rarely be enough to win on its own, though the odds of improvement to two pairs are good at less than 2 to 1. Hitting three of a kind is a 14 to 1 chance which, in itself, is probably less significant in determining whether to bet than the size of the pot and the amount a player has already contributed to it.

Winning positions

Having a strong hand after five cards obviously helps a player to determine how best to play the remaining three betting rounds. Anyone holding a high-ranking straight, a flush or possibly even a full house will not only be in a strong position to win but can escalate the betting if necessary to ward off potentially dangerous opposition.

The typical strategy to adopt when in this situation is to check, if opening the betting, or call, if this privilege falls to an opponent who decides to bet. This move is used to keep other opponents active in the game such that they will be more likely to call a big bet or raise on sixth street even if, by now, they know they are trailing. By delaying a big bet when holding a made hand, it is possible that an opponent's hand will improve sufficiently to win. On the whole, however, provided a player's assessment of developments throughout play is sound, such occurrences will be rare enough that slow-playing a hand in this way will regularly prove profitable.

Vulnerable leading hands

To be in possession of an invulnerable five-card hand on fifth street is unusual in the extreme. A more likely situation is that a player who currently leads will see plenty of evidence to suggest that this advantage could be temporary. Under these circumstances, an aggressive betting posture is generally advised in a bid to eliminate potentially dangerous opponents. For instance, a player with Ac, Jd in the hole and Jh, 8c, As on the board could easily be leading with two

Above: A player holding two pairs, aces and jacks, can expect to be in a very competitive position on fifth street with a hand that might prove good enough to win at the showdown. An aggressive betting posture is recommended unless there is any reason to suspect that an opponent may have the hand beaten already. Someone showing an open pair, for example, just might have a third card of the same rank for three of a kind.

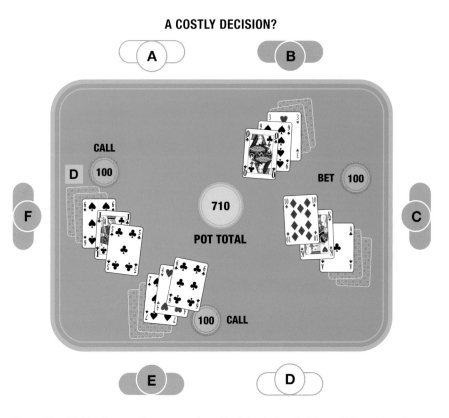

A COSTLY DECISION?

Above: The third betting round now sees player F call for 100, a decision which could easily prove costly given the improvement surely needed to win. By avoiding any aggressive betting moves so far, player F is advertising no strength at all and must be aware by now that a pair of fours is not enough. A flush might yet come good but this requires two of the remaining six unseen clubs in the deck (remember, player D folded the 7c earlier) on sixth and seventh street.

PLAYER B   PLAYER C   PLAYER E   PLAYER F

high pairs if the opposition's up cards reveal no obvious threat. Though a maximum bet is advised, any raise from an opponent would have to be taken very seriously and would call for a re-evaluation of the situation.

Unless the hand improves on sixth street, a more cautious approach will then be required since another maximum bet could trigger the same response from the opponent who is, at the very least, likely to call anyway with one card to come. Though the opponent may be bluffing with a weaker hand than that implied by the raise on fifth street, the warning signs are there to suggest that the player may need an A or J to win. In order to draw a relevant card, the player will want to keep the cost of doing so as cheap as possible, which means checking if in an early betting position and just calling if the opponent bets first.

Two cards to come

Assuming a player has identified that any drawing hand still has the chance to win with two cards to come, the strategy from fifth street onwards is to see those cards for the minimum outlay. Opponents will be attempting to make this as difficult as possible, a tactic that is much easier to achieve in pot-limit stud than in the fixed-limit game. Nevertheless, even when the likely cost of continuing to the showdown can be readily calculated, playing a drawing hand presents a challenge if there are several opponents still in contention. In these circumstances the best policy is to check or call but definitely not raise, particularly when in an early betting position. The danger of being drawn into a protracted betting war with the worst hand is far too great when in this situation and can result in the size of the pot tempting a player to continue unjustifiably in relation to the chances of actually winning.

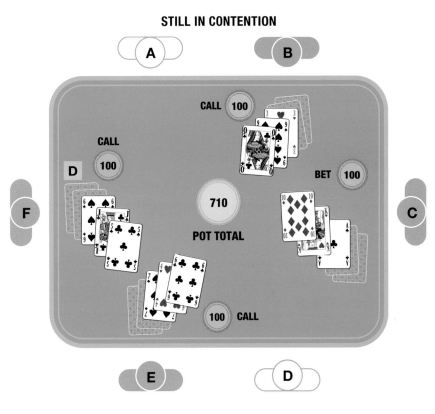

STILL IN CONTENTION

710

POT TOTAL

Above: After the exploratory raise in the previous round, player B just calls on this occasion, first because the Q has brought no improvement to the hand and, second, because the other three players remain involved. More importantly, even if player B pairs the A on sixth street, this could still prove inadequate given that player C could have paired the A and a higher card than a 9.

DRAWING DEAD
♦ ♣ ♥ ♠

All players strive to avoid persevering with a hand after fifth street when no available cards can improve it sufficiently to win – a situation known as 'drawing dead'. The number of hidden cards and a subtle betting strategy can help opponents to lay traps for the unwary. Novices often fail to spot the potential difficulty ahead when chasing drawing hands that, even if completed, could fall short of the mark. For example a player might continue betting on a straight draw, needing just one card to complete the hand, when an opponent with three diamonds showing has bet. A call may see the straight completed on sixth street and tempt the player into staying to the showdown where it will too often be beaten by the opponent's made flush or an equally successful draw for an even stronger hand.

Left: An open-ended straight draw after five cards might lure a player into drawing dead. Though a K or an 8 will complete the straight, it may not be worth pursuing if an opponent is showing three diamonds and has bet to infer that one hole card is also a diamond. Receiving a K on sixth street is devalued if the opponent is dealt a fourth diamond since the flush is almost certainly complete.

Sixth street

Even in a fairly loose fixed-limit game it is unusual for there to be many more than three players still contesting the pot on sixth street. A combination of the cards on display and the inferences drawn from the betting is generally enough to have caused anyone without a realistic chance of winning to fold beforehand.

Those at the table will have a fair idea of the quality of hands still in play and, for the players remaining in contention, the considerations are quite simple. A player who possesses what is clearly a winning, if not unbeatable, hand will be aiming to extract as many chips as possible from opponents who are now likely to stay to the showdown. Betting in a bid to eliminate them is extremely difficult at this stage, even in pot-limit stud where a sizeable bet may be interpreted as a bluff. Conversely, a player who holds a good hand but is uncertain whether it is strong enough to take the pot will hope to see seventh street for the minimum cost. This is only worthwhile if the cards that can improve a hand into a likely winner are available. This calculation is reasonably simple given that between a third and half the deck may, by now, have been exposed during play.

Extra bets

In fixed-limit stud there is little likelihood that a player can bet strongly enough to prevent any opponents on sixth street from calling for the final card. Anyone still taking part at this stage will have a reasonably accurate idea of the quality of hands apparently in opposition. As such, they will be more concerned with how their sixth card improves their prospects than with deciphering the subtleties of any betting move.

A player who is confident of leading on sixth street should bet, or raise if appropriate, in the expectation of being

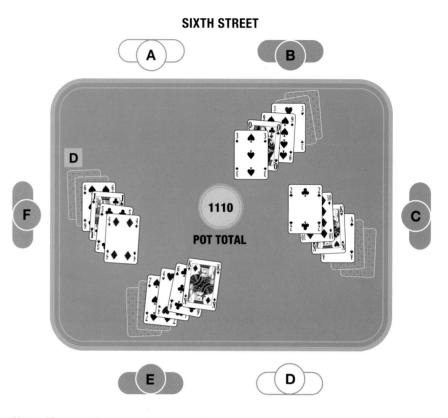

SIXTH STREET

1110

POT TOTAL

Above: After persisting with by far the worst hand, player F now takes the lead on sixth street with trip fours and just one card to come. Player B, meanwhile, has now found two pairs but knows that nines and threes, with four players competing, is unlikely to be good enough at the showdown. Players C and E both draw blanks.

PLAYER B   PLAYER C   PLAYER E   PLAYER F

called. Checking not only offers opponents a free opportunity to form a better hand, but also reduces the potential winnings on those occasions when the leading hand on sixth street retains its status at the showdown. The whole strategy for a player who is confident of being ahead is to try to induce as many extra bets from opponents as possible.

Checking and then raising a subsequent bet made by an opponent, a tactic known as 'checkraising', is sometimes worth considering but only if the player with the leading hand is confident that one or more opponents will bet on the strength of their cards. If so, then the player who initially checked can raise in the knowledge that anyone who has bet on sixth street will probably call the raise, rather than fold, even if they now suspect they are behind. The size of the pot relative to the amount required to call almost ensures this eventuality and satisfies the raiser's strategic aim of generating extra bets to maximize the profit on winning hands.

Seventh street

By seventh street a player's strategy in a fixed-limit game will be influenced by the number of opponents still involved and the player's position in the betting sequence. The final betting round will often be contested heads-up by just two players, in which case there is limited scope for subtle betting moves.

A player who is confident of victory and is set to act first should always bet to pressurize an opponent into calling with a beaten hand. Most opponents will do so in this situation provided there is still the slimmest of chances they might win, if only to indicate that they cannot be bluffed out of a pot at the end. When the player acting first harbours serious doubts about holding a successful hand, then a check is the only viable decision. There is nothing to be gained by betting since an opponent will fold if clearly beaten, but will probably raise if ahead, leading to the likely but unnecessary loss of additional chips when the player feels obliged to call.

In the same scenario against two or more opponents, a check is advised. Any bet with a weak hand is likely to be wasted since a caller will probably have a better hand. Also, there is always the risk that the bet could be raised and even re-raised. Then the player either folds, losing one bet, or calls with a good chance of losing even more last-round bets.

By checking first instead of betting, opponents may fear a checkraise move and might also check, so the showdown would come at no further cost. Likewise, any unraised bet in the final round might make a call justified in this position to trigger the showdown because the potential loss would be limited to a single additional bet. This provides a timely reminder that minimizing losses in poker is as important to long-term success as consistently winning large pots during a session.

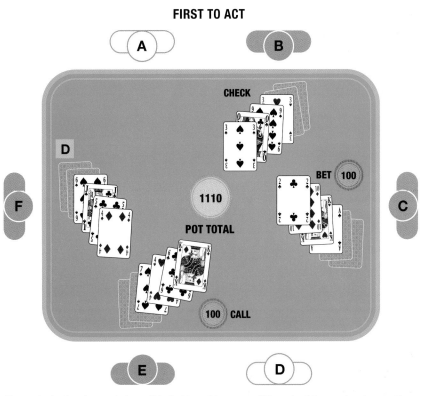

FIRST TO ACT

Above: In the fourth round player B is first to act because of the pair of threes showing and he checks, hoping to see seventh street for free. If the others remember player B's raise on fourth street and think it represented three nines, they might not bet for fear that player B is planning a checkraise with a full house. However, player C bets in support of the two pairs, kings and tens, although the K dealt to player E has reduced the chance of making a full house. Player E calls.

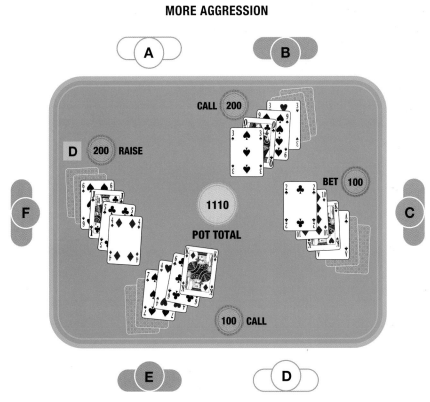

MORE AGGRESSION

Above: Player F now raises in support of the trip fours, a move that could represent to the opposition that the 4d has helped to complete a straight rather than three of a kind. Player B is now thinking that a full house is required to win, meaning that any of the nines and threes that are among the 31 cards he has yet to see must come on seventh street. The odds against this are about 7 to 1, making a call now almost obligatory as the pot odds are roughly the same.

Tournament play

Many poker players remain puzzled that despite its immense popularity, seven-card stud was passed over in favour of Texas Hold 'em as the game played for the WSOP world championship in the early 1970s. While the latter has come to dominate the tournament scene ever since, its rise to prominence owes much to the predilections of the professionals who contested those early contests. Their preference for the game is thought to have influenced Benny Binion's decision to adopt it for the WSOP.

However, pot-limit and fixed-limit seven-card stud tournaments soon became a fixture of the month-long WSOP event, while Europe's annual Poker EM, held in Vienna, is one of the most prestigious seven-card stud tournaments outside America. Pot-limit seven-card stud events are popular with experienced players, making them a risky prospect for the novice. For those considering a fixed-limit tournament, here are a few basic guidelines that may prove helpful.

Early stages

At the start of a multi-table tournament with seven or eight players per table, a cautious approach in support of only the best opening hands is the typical strategy. Anyone holding a strong hand will bet aggressively in the first round to capitalize on the early advantage by encouraging opponents to fold. To counter such aggression, only playing the best starting hands and drawing hands is therefore advisable to protect one's chip stack.

Any player holding a high pair after three cards is almost bound to continue to at least fifth street before re-assessing the situation, and will likely continue to bet aggressively until this stage to whittle away the opposition. With this in mind, only drawing hands featuring high-value cards should be considered an alternative since they offer

POT COMMITTED

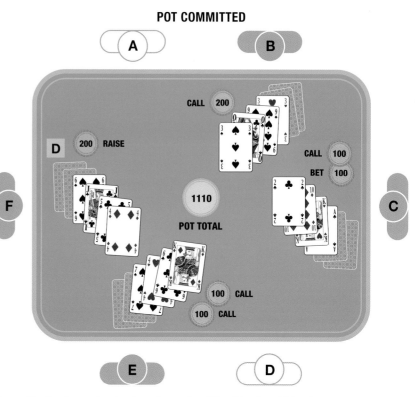

Above: The fourth round ends when players C and E call for the additional 100 chips. Both are under the impression that player F may well have formed a small straight and that they are likely to need help from the final card to emerge victorious. For player C, this means that only a K or a 10 will help while player E cannot be sure that a 5 will provide a straight good enough to win. However, having come this far, player E feels 'pot committed' and will obviously be reluctant to fold at this point for the sake of a few more chips with so much already invested in the pot.

SEVENTH STREET

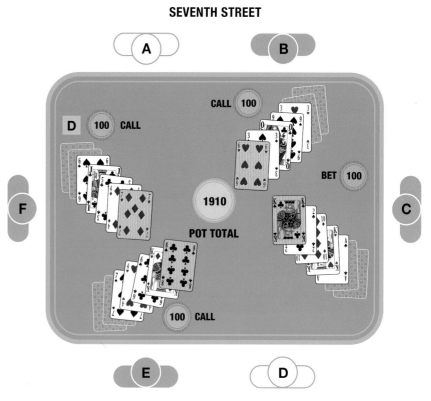

Above: Player B retains the honour to bet first in the final round but checks again, convinced that the two pairs are not enough. Player C, by contrast, bets 100 in support of the full house of kings over tens which is expected to prove the winner. For players E and F the moment of reckoning has arrived. Both have improved their low pairs into three of a kind, but the decision to keep calling in the earlier rounds has come back to haunt them. They call, as does player B.

other chances to win. A player holding As, Ks, 8s, for example, is justified in calling a raise from an opponent who has a Q showing and is representing a high pair since pairing the A or K may be enough to win, even if the flush does not materialize. Players must be wary of pursuing drawing hands blindly during the early stages of a tournament risking a regular loss of chips when survival is of most importance.

Middle stages

A tricky element of tournament play is that participants have no knowledge of their opponents' abilities or playing styles, so conservative play is sensible during the early stages. At a table of very conservative opponents, a player may be able to adopt a loose style by supporting marginal hands. For example a raise in late position to represent a large pocket pair when showing a 9 on third street could set up a winning bet on fourth street if another 9 or a picture card is dealt. A cautious opponent will suspect two pairs or three of a kind and will probably fold in the face of a possible full house developing unless there is a realistic chance of beating such a hand. Similarly, if there is plenty of action at the table with several players staying until fifth street, then it is wise to restrict one's involvement to hands which offer the most winning potential.

Apart from gauging the opponents' strength, another key factor governing strategy at this stage of the tournament will be the size of a player's chip stack. If low on chips, opponents are likely to raise with lesser hands than usual as they try to fashion a heads-up scenario that may eliminate the player from the event. Despite the pressure of being short on chips, having the patience to wait for a prime starting hand before committing oneself to a pot offers the best chance of surviving to the later stages.

SHOWDOWN

2310
POT TOTAL

Above: The showdown confirms that player C has won with the full house to claim the pot of 2,310 chips. This example shows the hands that can occur in seven-card stud, especially when several players stay to the showdown. Two pairs and three of a kind are often good enough to win, but the chances of these hands holding up is greater if the field is reduced by fifth street.

PLAYER B   PLAYER C   PLAYER E   PLAYER F

THE FINAL TABLE
♦ ♣ ♥ ♠

Stack size at the final table is the crucial in determining strategy. During the tournament, players in the leading chip positions can avoid getting involved in hands, while short-stacked opponents try to claw their way back into contention. Players with just enough chips for a handful of bets need to be similarly selective in which hands they play. The difference is that when dealt a reasonable hand, they must bet aggressively straight away.

A player has a better chance of winning when all-in on third street against one rival than betting all-in on fifth street against two or three. By the time the tournament is down to the last three or four players, the average value of the winning hand will drop while play is likely to be more aggressive. Stealing the antes with the first raise is a typical ploy and more bluffing is apparent, especially when a player's board cards suggest a strong hand.

The key to success at this stage lies in a player's ability to judge the situation and the opposition as much as the quality of hand to support.

TEXAS HOLD 'EM

Texas Hold 'em begins with the first player to the left of the dealer making a compulsory bet known as the small blind, after which the next player bets the big blind, usually set at the same level of the minimum bet for the first round, while the small blind is generally half this sum. The cards are dealt one at a time, face down, until each player has two cards which are referred to as their hole or pocket cards. A round of betting follows before the dealer reveals three cards, face up, on the table. This is called the 'flop'. Following the flop, a second betting round takes place and then a fourth card – the 'turn' – is dealt face up next to the flop, after which there is further betting, with the minimum bet permitted typically doubling at this point. The fifth and final face-up card, known as the 'river', is revealed by the dealer prior to the last round of betting. The objective is for players to make the best five-card poker hand possible from their two hole cards and the five community cards revealed on the table. Players may, if they wish, discount their hole cards entirely when finalizing their hand, in which case they are said to be 'playing the board', their hand comprising all five community cards.

If there is one poker variation that has contributed to the recent resurgence of interest in the game, it is without doubt Texas Hold 'em, often referred to simply as Hold 'em. The game is thought to have originated in Robstown, Texas, early in the 20th century, and was widespread in the southern states of America, although it was eclipsed in terms of popularity by seven-card stud. This state of affairs existed until Benny Binion decided to employ Texas Hold 'em as the variation to decide the WSOP World Champion in the early 1970s. The publicity surrounding the event created a demand for more poker tournaments and Texas Hold 'em established itself as the game of choice for such knockout events.

The most popular game

The legendary Johnny Moss once said that "chess is to checkers what Hold 'em is to draw or stud", underlining the complexities of the game that have made it so appealing to millions of players worldwide. Although the basic concepts of Texas Hold 'em are simple enough to grasp, playing it well takes courage, cunning and skill, particularly in pot-limit games (where maximum bets can be no higher than the total in the pot) or no-limit games (where players can bet all their chips at any time during play). These are the favoured betting structures for Texas Hold 'em tournaments, which have helped the game establish itself as a cultural phenomenon in the 21st century.

Television coverage of the tournament circuit and patronage from the stars of show business and sport has generated a stylish and fashionable image for the game that is attracting ever more interest. Consequently, Texas Hold 'em has acquired the status given to chess and bridge, with a wealth of books, feature articles and websites offering serious analytical appraisals of the game and how best to play it. In short, Texas Hold 'em is big business, while at the recreational level, it has revived interest in forming card schools and poker clubs, as newcomers to the game aim to discover the secrets behind its popularity.

Left: Johnny Moss, the first WSOP world champion and the man whose poker battle with Nicholas 'Nick the Greek' Dandolos in 1949 stimulated Benny Binion's desire to initiate the WSOP. Moss always considered Texas Hold 'em to be a more complex game than either draw or stud poker.

Online impact

Draw poker is traditionally the game to which beginners are exposed first, but in the Internet age, this situation is rapidly changing. Media coverage of Texas Hold 'em, together with the upsurge of interest that ensued, has coincided with the growth, since 1998, of online gaming sites that have been perfectly placed to meet the demand for ready access to poker. Texas Hold 'em attracts more players than any other online poker variation, and the ubiquitous nature of the game at present makes it likely that the next generation of poker players will cut their teeth on this game rather than on draw or stud.

Not all players appreciate the impact of the medium on the game itself, believing it to encourage poor poker habits in line with the speed at which decisions are made. Turbo tournaments, in which the blinds – the compulsory bets made by the two players to the immediate left of the dealer – are raised every two or three minutes, are popular at the lower-stake levels and will often be completed within the hour. However, the suggestion is that much of that popularity comes from the greater propensity for luck, rather than skill, to play a part. Bad calls do win on occasions and a poor player may need to be lucky just once with an all-in call in order to eliminate someone whose reading of the game is superior. For online players, the key point is that they should be open-minded in their analysis and not misread a lucky winning streak as evidence of skill.

Above: Behind the scenes at the TV production room during the *Ladbrokes Poker Million Masters* in 2004. Broadcast by Sky Sports in the UK, the event has become an integral part of the TV company's schedule since its inception in 2002. Each player's hand is always visible on camera, allowing the director to piece the action together in a suitably dramatic fashion to enhance a viewer's interest.

TELEVISED TOURNAMENTS
♦ ♣ ♥ ♠

After enthusiastic but limited attempts to convey the WSOP to a television audience during the 1970s, poker truly made its mark on the TV schedules from the late 1990s onwards. Cameras beneath the table enabled viewers to see the players' cards and, since tournaments almost invariably feature Texas Hold 'em, the game quickly became part of the mainstream consciousness. The enthusiasm for online gaming sites to sponsor tournaments staged for television has seen interest expand to the point where there are channels solely dedicated to broadcasting poker. Texas Hold 'em is the principal poker variation driving this interest, inspiring more viewers to play and improve their poker skills.

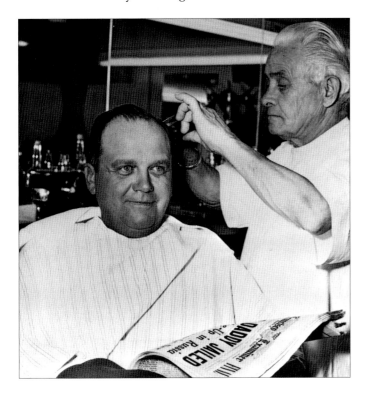

Left: Benny Binion, getting his hair cut for his court appearance, is the founder of legendary Binion's Horseshoe Casino, where all WSOP events were held until 2005. In 1964, he regained control of the Horseshoe Casino after selling his interest to cover his legal costs defending himself from tax evasion charges. As a convicted criminal, Benny could no longer hold a licence to run a gambling establishment. His sons Jack and Ted took over the operation of the casino. Benny remained on the payroll as a consultant.

Starting hands

In Texas Hold 'em, players are dealt just two cards at the start of play, yet even with so little initial information upon which to base a betting decision, this is still perhaps the most crucial moment of the game. Successful cash game players will probably see less than a third of all flops, and maybe as few as a fifth if they are strict in their choice of starting hands. Poorer players are usually much less disciplined in which hole cards they support, trusting in possibilities rather than probabilities. To an extent, this approach is conditioned by the factors motivating them to play; by definition, recreational or social players are keener to take part in the action and to view losses as the price paid for their entertainment.

Which of the 169 potential two-card combinations are worth playing depends on the likely value of the winning hand, as in all forms of poker. In Texas Hold 'em, a single high pair will often win the pot and hands such as two pairs or three of a kind (trips) are highly likely to do so, especially when the hand incorporates both hole cards. A player who holds pocket eights when a third 8 appears on the flop, the moment when the first three community cards are revealed, is in a powerful position due to the concealed strength of the hand. This is an obvious advantage compared to holding a pocket 8 that matches two eights on the flop when the implication behind any bet is much more easily read by opponents.

A straight or better will usually be good enough to win, but many hands of such potential are folded before they have a chance to be realized. This happens because unless the flop brings immediate promise of making the hand, the cost of drawing the cards for a straight or a flush, for example, can be made prohibitively expensive, relative to the odds against success.

STARTING HANDS

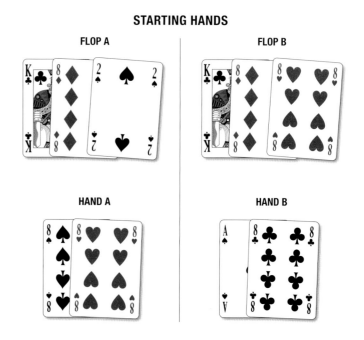

FLOP A   FLOP B

HAND A   HAND B

Above: Making three of a kind – trips – on the flop using a pocket pair and one board card, as here in hand A, puts a player in a better position than when making a similar hand with a pair on the board, as is shown in hand B. In the first example, only a player holding a pair of kings could be any threat, but an opponent holding A, K may bet in the belief that the top pair is leading. Whether a call or raise should follow depends on the willingness of the player holding trips to allow any opponents a chance to improve their hands before making a maximum bet. While making trips using just one pocket card is generally strong, any bet in support of the hand immediately suggests possession of either a K or an 8, which will normally be enough to end the hand.

Above: This hand of 7, 2 offsuit is popularly regarded as the worst possible two-card starting hand to be dealt in Texas Hold 'em and most players in receipt of these cards fold immediately. If dealt them while in the big blind, a player might choose to see the flop provided the betting has not been raised. Only if the flop then brings a minimum of two pairs could the player contemplate becoming seriously involved in any subsequent betting.

Right: In Texas Hold 'em, pairs of aces, kings or queens are seen as premium starting hands and players can raise before the flop, whichever betting structure is in operation. Medium pairs such as nines, eights and sevens are best played cheaply in the hope of hitting trips, and similarly for lower pairs. However, so many cards could appear on the flop to counterfeit a hand such as a pair of fours that players should beware of supporting them too strongly.

Pocket pairs

A pair will often be enough to take the pot, so being dealt a pair in the first two cards is advantageous, but players must beware of becoming too attached to the hand. Some pocket pairs are more valuable than others, with tens and above seen as playable wherever a player is sat in relation to the dealer. Pairs ranked 9 and below will usually need help from the board in the form of a matching card to prove successful, with the odds against making trips on the flop in the region of 8 to 1 against. This could justify calling a bet to see a cheap flop, but anyone with a pair lower than tens may find calling an opponent's raise much more difficult.

A raise is typically indicative of high cards being held, if not paired, meaning that any A, K, Q, J or 10 on the flop – any one of 20 cards – could immediately leave a player with pocket nines, for instance, trailing to a bigger pair. By contrast, a player who has pocket aces or kings has the chance to raise or re-raise any first-round bets, to defeat opponents and consolidate the early advantage.

This is crucial, since, while a pair of aces is the best possible hand before the flop, occurring once in every 220 deals, the board could supply a mixture of cards to help opponents. The more players who see the flop, the more card combinations are in play to blend with the board and render the aces second best. This is why most players advocate playing premium pocket pairs, such as aces, kings and queens, as aggressively as possible arguing that opponents must be made to bet heavily for a shot at beating them.

POCKET PAIRS

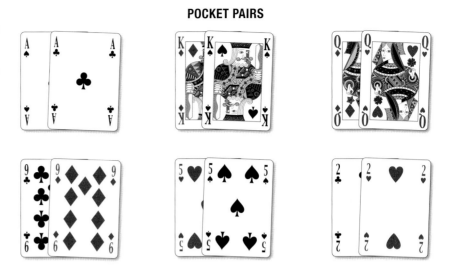

TOUCHING CARDS

♦ ♣ ♥ ♠

Two cards that are consecutive in rank – 'touching cards' – are valuable in Texas Hold 'em because, on 80 per cent of occasions, the board will contain at least three cards that could help form a straight, which, if held, is often good enough to win the pot. Two touching cards such as J, 10, for example, will fit with four different three-card combinations to form a straight, these being A, K, Q; K, Q, 9; Q, 9, 8 and 9, 8, 7. By comparison, even a hand such as A, 10 can only make a straight if K, Q, J appears on the board. Hands such as A, K and K, Q, although offering reduced chances of making the straight, are compensated by their potential for making the high pair, which is often enough to win at the showdown. Lower down the scale, hands such as 10, 9 and 5, 4 are generally regarded as poor starting hands and players who choose to play them usually do so when pre-flop betting is light. The inherent problem in playing low connecting cards is that when they do make straights, they may be at the wrong end of the spectrum. If the board contains 6, 7, 8, for example, then the player holding the 5, 4 has the low or 'ignorant end' of the straight and is outranked by anyone with 10, 9 or 9, 5. Similarly, K, Q, J on the board provides a straight for a player with 10, 9, but a holding of A, 10 will prove superior.

Above: Hands that feature touching cards offer straight opportunities given that the five board cards will include three cards to a straight 80 per cent of the time. A hand such as the A, K can only make a straight with the Q, J, 10 on the board but the high-ranking cards are beneficial. The 9, 8 combination, however, will blend with four different three-card combinations to make a straight, although there is the potential for it to be second best. The Q, J, 10 combination to form one possible straight could easily form a higher example for a player holding A, K or K, 9.

Suited cards

Holding two suited cards after the deal offers a player possibilities of a flush, although these are best realized when just three cards of the relevant suit are on the board, rather than four. Holding Ks, Qs is much more beneficial if the board reads Ad, 9s, 8s, 6d, 4s, rather than Ad, 9s, 8s, 6s, 4s. In the first instance, it is plausible that an opponent contesting the pot holds the As and a card of a different suit, thus the resulting flush represents the best hand. But with four spades on the board, an opponent with the As would obviously take the pot. This underlines another benefit in holding the A in any suit, and highlights the possibilities of playing any A-suited combination, although the A, 9; A, 8; A, 7 and A, 6 hands are weaker. They do not offer the added benefit of blending with a three-card combination on the board to make a straight.

Flushes are strong hands in Texas Hold 'em, but they have to be played with a degree of caution, since players will often have to see the turn and the river card in order to fill them. A flush draw can be expensive for a player to pursue when an opponent has read the hand correctly. Although there is a 40 per cent chance that the five board cards will feature at least three of the same suit, there are four suits, reducing the relevant chances of any suited pairing matching the board to 1 in 10. Furthermore, the chances of a flush being made on the flop when in possession of suited hole cards are fractionally less than 1 per cent but, although such a hand is powerful, exploiting it to the full can be testing, especially without the A. Betting with such a hand will usually win the pot, making a small profit, however slow-playing it always runs the risk of someone else securing a higher-value flush or, if the board subsequently pairs, a full house.

FILLING A FLUSH

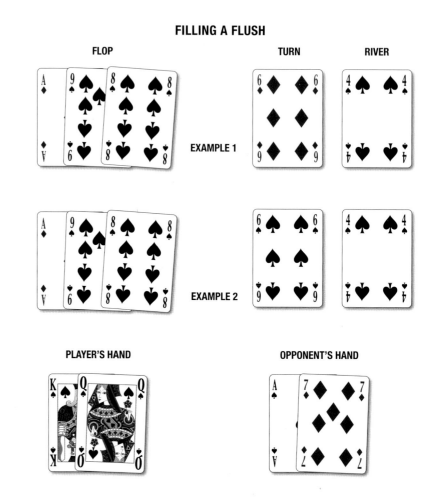

Above: This illustration highlights the potential problems that arise when holding suited pocket cards but not the A. In the first example, the player holding Ks, Qs has two chances to hit a winning spade although the opponent, who holds the leading hand on the flop and the turn with a pair of aces, could make it expensive to stay in the game. In the second example, the turn card puts the player in front with a flush but even an all-in bet might not persuade the opponent holding the As to fold, with potentially disastrous consequences if the river brings a fourth spade.

Above: An opening hand of K, 9, often referred to as 'Lassie' or 'Rin-Tin-Tin'. The hand is more valuable when suited, as in this example, but it can be tricky to play it well. Doyle Brunson is one professional who dislikes it because too many of the cards that might help it develop into a strong hand are likely to do the same for an opponent. Pairing the K, for instance, is of no help if someone else holds a K with a higher kicker, which is a very plausible prospect.

PLAYING MEDIUM PAIRS
FLOP A

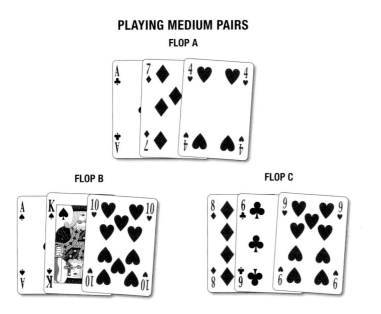

FLOP B
FLOP C

PLAYER'S HAND

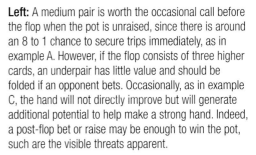

Left: A medium pair is worth the occasional call before the flop when the pot is unraised, since there is around an 8 to 1 chance to secure trips immediately, as in example A. However, if the flop consists of three higher cards, an underpair has little value and should be folded if an opponent bets. Occasionally, as in example C, the hand will not directly improve but will generate additional potential to help make a strong hand. Indeed, a post-flop bet or raise may be enough to win the pot, such are the visible threats apparent.

Marginal hands

The dubious potential of mid-ranking pairs has already been explained, as they can too often become impotent after the flop. A hand such as a pair of sevens can be played when in the big blind since, if nobody raises, a player in that position can check the betting and see the flop at no further cost having already committed the required chips in the pot. If there is no help from the flop in the shape of a 7 or a low straight-draw possibility, the hand should probably be folded in the face of the first bet.

Touching cards ranked J or lower, even if suited, pose similar problems. Whether to play them will depend on the opposition and the situation in a game, but they are rarely powerful enough to call

any pre-flop raise. The flops that can help marginal hands are less likely to appear and the danger is that when they do, an opponent's hand may improve even more.

Poor prospects

More than half the possible two-card combinations are simply never worth playing by anyone with pretensions to being a profitable player. Picture cards with unsuited low cards such as Kh, 2d or Js, 6c have little merit when one considers the composition of the board. They need very specific flops to fall in order to warrant continued support. For example a player holding Kh, 2d when the flop is Kd, 10s, 7c has a top pair but with a very weak kicker. If an opponent bets, the obvious conclusion is that a pair of kings is being represented, it being unusual for a player, holding 9s, 8d for instance, to open the betting in pursuit of a straight draw. This is terminal for the K, 2 since any opponent holding a K cannot hold a kicker lower than 2 and so cannot be losing, making it difficult to withstand any aggressive move. Similar comments apply to a pair of twos that can only be confidently supported after the flop should another 2 be dealt.

POTENTIAL DANGER
FLOP A
FLOP B

FLOP C
PLAYER'S HAND

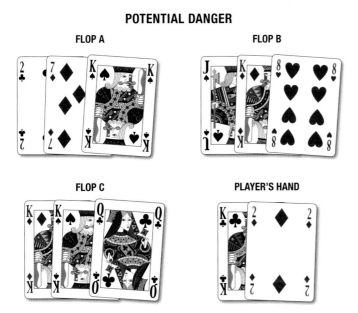

Above: A weak hand such as K, 2 offsuit needs too much help from the board to be seriously competitive. Flop A offers two pairs, which could warrant a maximum post-flop bet to dissuade callers who fear trips. Yet it could still lose to another poor starting hand of K, 7. Flop B is more dangerous because holding a top pair with a weak kicker is inviting trouble. Any opponent who holds a K with a better kicker is immediately in front, and K, J offsuit could be in opposition. Even making trips as shown in flop C could see the K, 2 against the final K with a higher kicker.

Before the flop

Having assessed the promise of their opening two cards, players have to consider the other factors at work when deciding whether to bet or fold before the flop. Of these, the number of opponents, their position relative to the dealer, and the nature of the game will be the most vital.

A restrained, low-stakes fixed-limit game between ten players may well see five or six calling to see the flop if it is habitually unraised. By contrast, pot-limit and no-limit Texas Hold 'em could see sizeable raises before the flop, as players try to test the resolve of their opponents and reduce the competition. Only by understanding the context of a particular game can a player form a strategy for the hand in progress.

When betting to see the flop, players should be clear on what they need in order to win, while retaining the discipline to fold if the flop brings no encouragement. Loose players are inclined to see too many flops with poor or marginal hands, the likely result of this indiscriminate policy being a steady reduction in their chips as the game unfolds.

Early betting decisions

How to proceed once the cards are dealt will depend on the character of the players and their motives. This underlines the value of observing, to build up a picture of the hands opponents play and the betting moves they make. In a tight game featuring plenty of folding before the flop, it can pay to be flexible regarding which starting hands to support. A raise before the flop, with a marginal hand, may even be enough to steal the blinds occasionally in a game where opponents are reluctant to play with anything less than excellent cards. They are more likely to respect a pre-flop raise and assume it indicates a high pair or A, K until it is proved otherwise.

In a hectic game where several players routinely see the flop, a more patient strategy is prudent. Playing only the stronger starting hands would conserve chips for those times when a player wishes to maximize the return on investment, having found a winner. Opponents who are preoccupied with their own game may not notice the implications behind a cautious player's participation in the hand until it is too late.

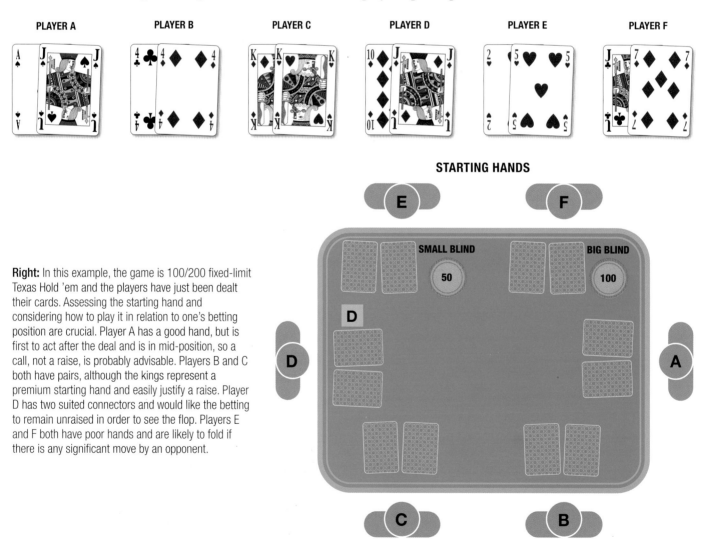

Right: In this example, the game is 100/200 fixed-limit Texas Hold 'em and the players have just been dealt their cards. Assessing the starting hand and considering how to play it in relation to one's betting position are crucial. Player A has a good hand, but is first to act after the deal and is in mid-position, so a call, not a raise, is probably advisable. Players B and C both have pairs, although the kings represent a premium starting hand and easily justify a raise. Player D has two suited connectors and would like the betting to remain unraised in order to see the flop. Players E and F both have poor hands and are likely to fold if there is any significant move by an opponent.

Positional play

In Texas Hold 'em, a player's position during the betting round is more significant than in any other poker game. The earlier a player has to act, the more difficult it is to control the betting given the lack of information upon which to base any decision. This affects the quality of the starting hand a player can expect to support before the flop, with hands that are virtually unplayable in an early betting position becoming much more attractive when on the dealer button. The dealer is always last to act in the betting rounds that succeed the flop and so has much more information from opponents regarding the quality of their hands. For example, when holding K, J offsuit and seated next to the big blind (who is in second position, clockwise from the dealer), a call might seem reasonable, but the player is vulnerable to subsequent raises from opponents. Since the initial reaction would be to assume such opponents hold a high pair or an A with a good kicker – A, K; A, Q; A, J, for example – the potential of the K, J is immediately devalued. The decision is whether to fold for the loss of a single bet or risk another bet in the knowledge that the hand is probably already losing. The problem in doing this is that cards that may help on the flop could easily improve an opponent's hand as well in this situation. Pair the K alone and an opponent with A, K or K, Q is still ahead, while a flop of K, J, 10 for two pairs could be losing to someone with A, Q for a straight.

Holding the same hand on the dealer button, however, offers much more scope, since, if nobody raises, a call will probably be enough to see the flop. This allows the player to gauge the inferences behind opponents' post-flop bets without having to risk any further chips. Premium hands such as the high pairs and A, K can be played in any position, almost without exception. As a general rule, the earlier a player's position relative to the dealer, the stronger the starting hand is normally required to be.

Below: A pair of twos, sometimes called deuces or ducks. While being dealt a pair in Hold 'em is generally advantageous, a pair of twos should be played as inexpensively as possible since making trips on the flop is the likeliest route to victory. Calling a pre-flop raise with them is unwise and, if failing to hit three of a kind on the flop, the hand is probably worthless.

PRE-FLOP BETTING

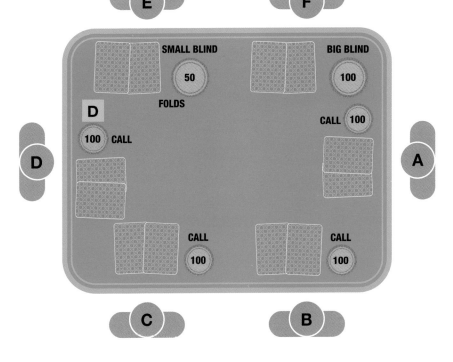

Right: Player A's decision to err on the side of caution by calling encourages player B to call with the pair of fours, although a raise from player A might well have seen the small pair folded instead. Player C has the chance to raise but decides instead to disguise the strength of the hand with a call. This is a questionable move since it could easily allow one of the weaker hands to improve past it. Player D now has the chance to call as well and player F checks on the big blind, leaving five players to see the flop. Player E's hand is too poor to be worth calling for the extra 50 chips and is folded.

Playing the flop

Although deciding which starting hands to play is crucial, it is the flop that defines whether or not such decisions were justified. Strong two-card holdings can easily be compromised while poor hands will, on occasion, become unbeatable, given the right flop. When each player can see five of the seven cards from which they will ultimately form their hand, they can quickly deduce the best that they can achieve and, most importantly, whether that will be enough to win the pot. However, it is rare for a player to hold the nuts at this stage, from which it can be understood that leading hands may yet be beaten, while weak hands could still improve sufficiently to win.

This volatility is what makes Texas Hold 'em such an appealing and challenging game to play. In terms of strategy, factors such as position, the betting structure in use and the playing styles of opponents are still of paramount importance. But with more information now available in the form of the flop, players are able to calculate how many of the cards remaining unseen might help or hamper their chances of victory. Any post-flop strategy, therefore, should always begin with an assessment of the probabilities that emerge from the cards in play. Only then can the actions of opponents be viewed from the proper perspective as each player attempts to outwit the others and secure the pot.

Strong play

Each deal offers a completely different scenario, so knowing how best to exploit any given situation depends on a player's ability to assimilate all the information available and act accordingly. Skilful players are better able to strike a balance between aggression and caution after the flop and choose a strategy that fits the specific situation. In this regard, strong play may involve folding a good hand in response to a large bet as much as managing the pot when holding a guaranteed winner. For example a player holding pocket kings who raised before the flop and elicited one caller will be extremely wary if the

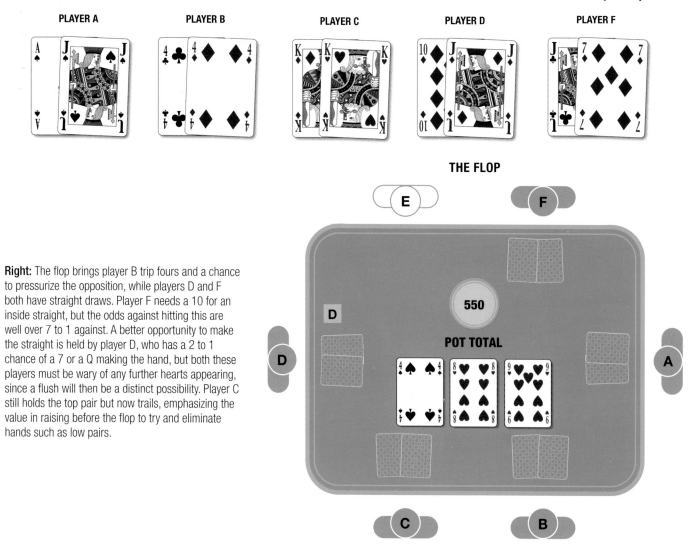

Right: The flop brings player B trip fours and a chance to pressurize the opposition, while players D and F both have straight draws. Player F needs a 10 for an inside straight, but the odds against hitting this are well over 7 to 1 against. A better opportunity to make the straight is held by player D, who has a 2 to 1 chance of a 7 or a Q making the hand, but both these players must be wary of any further hearts appearing, since a flush will then be a distinct possibility. Player C still holds the top pair but now trails, emphasizing the value in raising before the flop to try and eliminate hands such as low pairs.

flop shows an A but no K. Any bet from the opponent surely indicates possession of an A and good players will fold the kings there and then. However appealing the hand was after the deal, it is no stronger in this situation than any other pocket pair lower than aces.

Conversely, raising before the flop to represent an A and then putting in a big bet when one materializes on the flop is powerful play, particularly if opponents are known to call pre-flop raises with marginal hands. Unless they can beat a pair of aces, calling a bet in this situation is extremely difficult for anyone without an A, even if they have the potential to improve their hand. Given that the typical policy in Texas Hold 'em is to bet with leading hands and force opponents to pay for the cards that may win them the pot, the occasional bluff representing an A can be a positive move when used sparingly.

Weak play

Instances of weak play are not always restricted to players in possession of poor hands, either before or after the flop. Most experts would advocate raising before the flop with a pair of aces in a ten-player game, for example, since to enable several opponents the opportunity to see the flop cheaply decreases the hand's effectiveness. Any pair on the flop could easily provide an opponent with three of a kind and render the aces impotent. This highlights one of the guiding principles of Texas Hold 'em, which determines that players should never become emotionally attached to a powerful starting hand that is diminished in strength after the flop.

On the whole, however, weak play generally consists of players making the wrong decision in relation to the current state of their hand. Those who decide not to bet when in a leading position always run the risk of allowing an opponent to overtake them at negligible cost. Nevertheless, the poorest betting strategy is to continue calling opponents' bets when the possibility of obtaining the card or cards required to win simply does not justify remaining involved in the hand. Pots that are won on the occasions when a player is lucky enough to draw the relevant cards will very rarely compensate for the amount of money lost in similar circumstances during the game.

Above: A pair of aces in the hole, sometimes called 'pocket rockets', is the best starting hand available in Texas Hold 'em. Despite the initial advantage enjoyed when holding pocket aces, success cannot be guaranteed which is why most players dealt the hand will raise before the flop as with any other high-ranking pair.

Right: Player F is first to act and checks, as does player A, who has two overcards to the flop but little encouragement to pursue the hand further. Any significant betting might be enough to prompt a fold, given the straight and flush draws made possible by the flop. Player B bets with the three fours, but knows this may still not be enough to force opponents out of the game. Were this a pot-limit or no-limit game, then a much bigger bet would be possible to drive out any drawing hands, but, as it stands, player C is able to call, in the belief that the pair of kings could still be winning. This also allows player D to call, since the current pot odds of over 7 to 1 exceed the 3 to 1 against drawing one of the six cards that will make the straight, these being the Q and 7 in any suit but hearts.

POST-FLOP BETTING

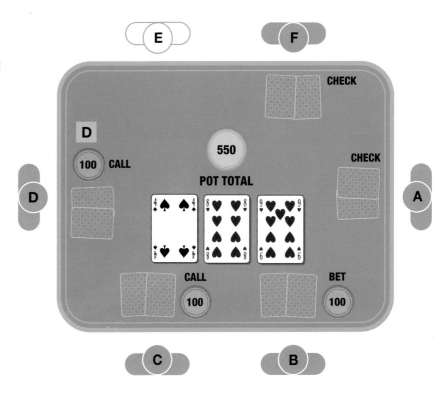

Assessing chances

The three community cards on the flop provide the most immediate opportunity for a player to evaluate the chances of success prior to the beginning of the second betting round. Those players who are in the later positions have time to factor their opponents' betting decisions into the equation once the action is under way, but the cards themselves provide the earliest clues regarding whether to play or not.

On occasions where the flop offers no help at all, the usual recommendation is to fold at the first sign of any betting. A hand of 9d, 9s, for instance, is unlikely to withstand a flop of Ad, Kh, 10c when an opponent bets to indicate possession of at least a high pair. Apart from the possibility of someone holding another A, K or 10 (constituting nine cards), the appearance of a Q or J on the board (a further eight cards) would simply enhance the possibility of a straight being made. In this situation, while the pair of nines may be winning, it is highly unlikely with so many cards in the deck working unfavourably. Only seeing nines on the turn and river – when the fourth and fifth and final community cards are dealt respectively – can guarantee victory and the odds against this are 1,000 to 1, so the rational decision would be to fold. This example illustrates that a player should always be assessing the probability of a hand improving enough to win the pot, rather than for it merely to improve.

Calculating outs

On the vast majority of occasions, the flop will not furnish a player with the nuts, and, when it does, the board cards will probably nullify any attempt to capitalize on the hand. To take an extreme example, a player holding a pair of queens when the flop is Q, Q, 7 faces an obvious problem in persuading opponents to call a bet. Consequently, players will typically have to calculate the number of outs – cards that can help them keep or obtain the winning hand – available in the deck. For the most part, players who require help from the board will typically be seeking just one of several cards on either the turn or the river.

The more cards that help, the better the opportunities with the tipping point being 13 or 14 cards, since having this many working in a player's favour offers an even-money chance of success. Those drawing to flushes or open-ended straights usually have eight or nine cards that will make the hand, the odds against which are 2 to 1. Any player with 14 or more unseen cards in the deck that will help secure victory is favourite to win.

Below: While player F folded, the escalating size of the pot tempted player A to call on the flop and the turn card – Ks – now offers the chance of an unlikely winning flush. It also illustrates the dynamic nature of Texas Hold 'em, with the lead changing hands once again, as well as highlighting the need for players with leading hands to bet aggressively in an effort to eradicate such potential threats. Player C is now in a very strong position, but may still not be able to bet enough to induce the others to fold.

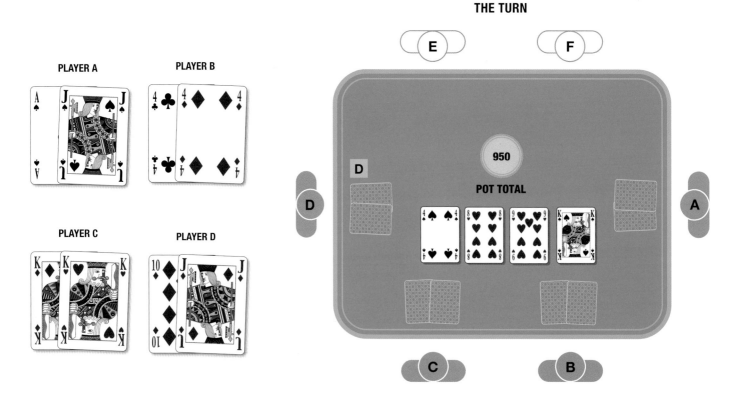

THE TURN

PLAYER A PLAYER B

PLAYER C PLAYER D

Common errors

Mistakes made by players after the flop tend to fall into two categories. They either overvalue their hands and call optimistically despite their poor chance of winning, or they simply pay too little attention to the betting and fail to grasp the implications behind it. This can befall those with leading hands as well as those who need cards to win. Anyone holding Jc, Jd when the flop reads As, Jh, 9c, for example, may be inclined to slow-play the hand, since trip jacks is very strong and would be second only to a player with pocket aces. However, should any K, Q, 10, 8 or 7 be seen on the turn, then an opponent could conceivably make a straight. That is a total of 20 unseen cards that could beat the hand, while any A could do the same if an opponent has an A with the remaining J for a bigger full house.

With so many cards promising potential danger, a maximum bet is advised to force opponents out of the pot. Waiting until the turn card before betting could prove too late to have any effect, by which time the promise of the trip jacks has dissolved.

Above: The scene after the flop as a player hits three Js. Despite the apparent strength of the hand, any one of 20 cards on the turn could conceivably provide an opponent with a straight. In recognition of this, it would be best for the player holding the jacks to bet the maximum now to encourage opponents with straight draws to fold. If the bet is big enough, even players who have paired the A on the flop may think twice before calling.

Right: Undeterred by the calls in the previous round, player B bets 200, this being the minimum for the final two rounds, but is raised by player C, whose bet indicates that the K has proved helpful. For player D, the cost of calling is too prohibitive, since the pot is now offering less than 4 to 1 when the chance of hitting a winning card on the river has risen to over 10 to 1 against. This is because only four cards – the Q and 7 in clubs and diamonds – can now secure a potential winning hand without filling a flush. Player A, however, has a 4 to 1 chance of catching another spade for the nut flush, but must be concerned that, with two evidently strong hands in play, a call of 400 chips may yet be raised again by players B and C.

BETTING ON THE TURN

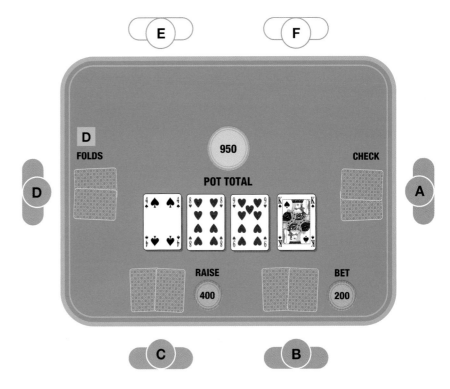

Leading hands

Holding a leading hand after the flop is obviously advantageous, but playing the hand correctly in order to realize its winning potential is still a challenging proposition. On the occasions when a player makes a powerful hand on the flop, such as a full house or a straight flush, the objective is to manage the pot and extract as much as possible from opponents. In this case, checking on the flop, and perhaps on the turn card, is often the only way to induce a bet from opponents, who, if their hands have improved, might assume that the board has not helped other players at all.

Making an unbeatable hand – the nuts – on the flop is a rare occurrence, and most leading hands, no matter how strong, remain vulnerable to defeat. A player with Kc, Qs, for instance, will probably be leading if the flop cards are Kd, 8d, 7s, but if several opponents call a bet advertising the pair of kings, then it is likely that straight and flush draws are being pursued at least. If so, the high pair could be beaten by any one of 29 cards that could complete an opponent's straight or flush, added to which any A, 8 or 7 in suits other than diamonds could also threaten defeat. With up to 80 per cent of the cards working against the pair of kings, the likelihood is that the hand will lose in a showdown. If some aggressive betting on the flop cannot eliminate all opposition under these circumstances, then caution is definitely advocated as the game progresses.

Drawing hands

Whether in possession of a leading hand or one that is trailing, requiring one of several cards to bring about certain victory after the flop is an integral part of Texas Hold 'em. The term 'drawing hands', however, is usually associated with those players who need one card on the turn or river in order to improve sufficiently past a leading hand to win. Players holding suited or connecting cards repeatedly encounter this situation as they try to draw the one card needed to complete a flush or a straight.

In general, the strategy behind playing such hands is to remain in the game as cheaply as possible, since, with two chances to hit the required card, there are obviously two more possibly expensive betting rounds to negotiate. Yet the potential for straights and flushes and full houses when there is a pair on the flop, is all too apparent to those with leading hands. Opponents currently holding the best hand can be expected to try forcing out the drawing hands by betting, so a keen eye on the existing and implied pot odds is advisable when in this situation.

By way of warning, it should be emphasized that more chips are lost by players fruitlessly pursuing drawing hands than in any other aspect of the game. This covers not just hands that fail to improve, but those that do realize their potential, only to secure the runner-up position.

Right: In the event, both players A and B call the raised bet of 400 chips, the former still hoping the flush draw will materialize while the latter is working on the assumption that player C has made no more than two pairs. The river gives player A the nuts since the A-high flush in spades is the best possible hand now available given the board cards, the chances against which were 24 to 1 against occurring when the flop was revealed. Now a bet from player A is absolutely essential, since it is the only way of tempting opponents into putting more chips into a pot they cannot win. Checking in the hope of being able to re-raise later runs the risk of seeing everyone do the same; the pot will still be won, but the profit will be reduced.

THE RIVER

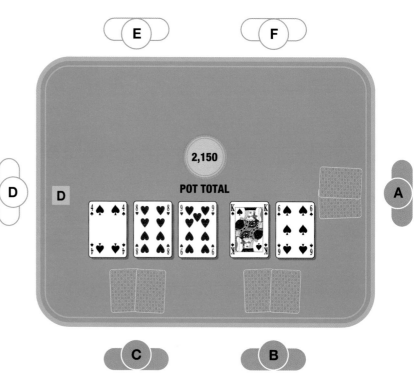

PLAYER A   **PLAYER B**

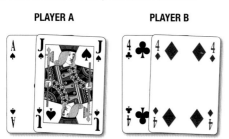

Chasing hands

Hands that need two cards to realize their potential – chasing hands – should ordinarily be folded unless everyone checks on the flop. Expecting two cards to fall conveniently on the turn and river is extremely optimistic and players in such situations should usually fold if there is any significant betting. A player holding Qh, Jh when the flop is Kd, 5s, 6h, for example, would be ill-advised to pursue the flush, since there is only a four per cent chance of the next two cards bringing running hearts. Odds of 24 to 1 against this occurring virtually guarantee that the pot odds will never justify supporting a chasing hand.

When they do win, it is usually in a light betting heat in which all players have poor hands. An example would be when a player holds Kc, 9c and the flop reads Qs, 4c, 8d. Should nobody bet on the flop and the turn card is the Jc, then the player has a 4 to 1 chance of seeing another club on the river for the flush, odds which might justify a third-round call if the pot odds are appealing.

Above: An example of a typical chasing hand with the player holding Q, J suited, realistically needing help on both the turn and the river cards to offer a possible winning opportunity. Two more hearts will provide a flush while an A and 10 or 10 and 9 will complete a straight, and these are hands that could easily prove best. Unless there is little or no betting after the flop, chasing two cards for a winning hand is rarely worthwhile since the pot odds rarely justify it.

THE CONCLUSION

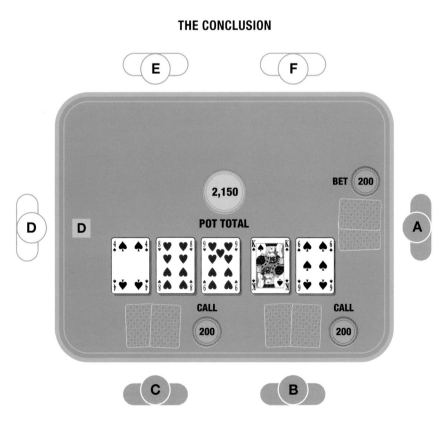

Left: Player A bets with impunity, knowing that players B and C must have reasonably strong hands and might call just to be certain a bluff is not being executed. Both are aware that player A initially checked on the flop and the turn but later called the bets made in both rounds, indicating that a flush could now be held. However, with both of them holding trips, they decide to call, with player C, particularly, regretting that the earlier advantage could not be pressed home. Had the game been a no-limit contest, an all-in move by player C after the K appeared on the turn may well have forced player A out of the hand.

PLAYER C

Post-flop strategies

Players who are sufficiently enamoured of their cards to consider betting will visualize the potential for winning. To achieve this, players will require their visions to be coloured by some strategic thinking concerning the probability of various outcomes during play. Although an assessment of the cards on display is important, the style and betting structure of the game, as well as the quality of the opposition will also influence any viable strategy.

Irrespective of the cards and probabilities in play, it is always easier to call a bet from a serial bluffer in a fixed-limit game than it is to call a raise by someone who normally folds nine hands in every ten while playing pot-limit Texas Hold 'em. For champion Doyle Brunson, the key elements in any post-flop strategy are the intangible qualities of patience and self-discipline, particularly when playing fixed-limit Texas Hold 'em. The pot-limit and no-limit games do permit greater licence to prosecute bold post-flop play via large raises and credible bluffs, but having the patience to wait – for the right cards against the right opponent and when in the right position – remains an asset.

Varying approaches

The fluid and volatile nature of Texas Hold 'em provides enough uncertainty over the outcome of most hands that players need to adopt a range of varied strategic approaches when playing the flop. In early position with the leading hand, the recommendation is generally to bet. Allowing opponents free cards is only advisable when a player is confident they can do little damage. If the flop offers a probable winning hand, however, a checkraise after the flop may be in order when one or two opponents can confidently be expected to bet. If they fold after the raise, the pot is won, but

THE DEALER BUTTON STEAL

PLAYER C

Above: When a pot is unraised before the flop and the action is checked around to the dealer afterwards, it will often mean that the flop has helped nobody much at all. Should opponents show weakness in this way, a bet from player C, in this instance, could be enough to take the pot. By representing an A in the hole to make the high pair, opponents who have no A and no help from the flop will find it immensely difficult to justify calling. Such a move is more likely to succeed when the player can bet substantially in order to underline the threat, making this a more viable tactic in pot-limit or no-limit Texas Hold 'em.

Above: A cashier at the Commerce Casino in Los Angeles counts out an equal number of chips for each player participating in the World Poker Tour Invitational event. Exposure to the styles and techniques of the top professionals via televised events such as this has helped confirm Texas Hold 'em as the poker game of choice for most players.

should the motive behind the raise be doubted, they will probably call and may well feel committed to the pot thereafter, despite the chance of drawing to a beaten hand.

In later positions, players have the opportunity to take a few liberties on occasions, especially when betting is light. Should the action be checked around the table, for example, the player on the dealer button may be able to steal the pot with a finely judged bet. If a flop of Ah, 9d, 4c invokes no response from others, then a bet to represent an A in the hole for the top pair is perfectly reasonable, provided nobody had raised before the flop. Here, a 'feeler' bet will win the pot or expose the fact that any caller probably has an A, which, if combined with a weak kicker, could explain the previous reluctance to bet.

The key to which strategy or betting style to adopt lies in closely observing the opposition. In a game featuring several cautious players, a little loose play can reap benefits by playing on their fears. Equally, in a game with inexperienced or loose players inclined to call at every opportunity, a more conservative and studied approach is recommended.

BLUFFING IN THE BIG BLIND

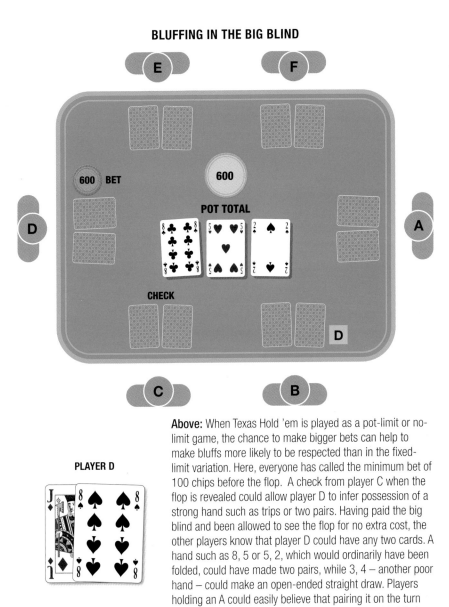

PLAYER D

Above: When Texas Hold 'em is played as a pot-limit or no-limit game, the chance to make bigger bets can help to make bluffs more likely to be respected than in the fixed-limit variation. Here, everyone has called the minimum bet of 100 chips before the flop. A check from player C when the flop is revealed could allow player D to infer possession of a strong hand such as trips or two pairs. Having paid the big blind and been allowed to see the flop for no extra cost, the other players know that player D could have any two cards. A hand such as 8, 5 or 5, 2, which would ordinarily have been folded, could have made two pairs, while 3, 4 – another poor hand – could make an open-ended straight draw. Players holding an A could easily believe that pairing it on the turn might also fill a straight for their opponent in the big blind.

BLUFFING OPPORTUNITIES
♦ ♣ ♥ ♠

As mentioned previously, bluffing on the flop in a fixed-limit game is hampered by the inability of players to bet sufficient amounts to intimidate opponents into laying down their hands. In this respect, carving out a reputation as someone who only raises with a top-quality hand can help a player to sneak through an occasional bluff, perhaps, when the risk of being called is generally high. Other betting structures, however, do improve the chances of bluffs being successful, since larger bets are permitted – the impact of this is twofold. First, any pot-sized bet after the flop makes the cost of calling more expensive, and second, the pot odds facing anyone wishing to call are immediately rendered much less attractive. Since a bet from a player in early position usually advertises strength, a pot-sized bluff by the player in the big blind becomes a possibility. Assuming there were no pre-flop raises, a forceful bet from the big blind when the flop reads 8c, 5h, 2s, for example, could easily persuade opponents with high cards to fold. Having already paid the obligatory bet to see the flop, but no more, opponents know that the player could have made a pair or even two pairs with cards that ordinarily would have been folded, such as 8, 5 or 5, 2. Even someone holding an overpair to the board will be wary of calling, given that any 8, 5 or 2 on the turn just might provide the big blind with three of a kind. Opportunities such as this may be rare, but there are times when they can be exploited, especially when opponents are betting timidly.

The art of deception

The ability to deceive opponents is an integral part of the game, which is why bluffing and varying one's betting style is so vital. The aim is to create doubt in the minds of opponents regarding the meaning behind any bet. If a bluff fails, opponents may consider it the tactic of a loose and reckless player, an image that may be exploited later when a strong hand develops.

In Texas Hold 'em, the capacity for the flop to offer potential to several players generates many opportunities to practise the art of deception. For example a flop of Ad, 3d, 10s presents the chance of a high straight, a low straight or a flush being realized, added to which anyone matching the board with their hole cards for a pair of aces, two pairs or three of a kind will almost certainly be keen to see the turn. Representing any one of these hands with a call or even a small raise could lay the foundations for success. Should any A, 10 or 3 be dealt on the turn, then a large bet would signal three of a kind or a full house has been made, making it difficult for those still needing a card to call. If the card is the 10d specifically, even someone with a made flush might baulk if having to call a large bet against a possible full house, while any opponents still drawing to a straight will definitely think they are beaten.

Using the flop in this way enables players to pick up pots occasionally, without necessarily having the cards to win. The one danger lies in representing a hand that is already held by an opponent, since betting as though holding pocket aces, for example, will prove costly should an opponent actually have pocket aces.

Right: Marlon Brando shuffles the deck in *A Streetcar Named Desire* (1951). Adapted from the Tennessee Williams play, the film features several scenes in which Stanley Kowalski (Brando) and his friends play poker.

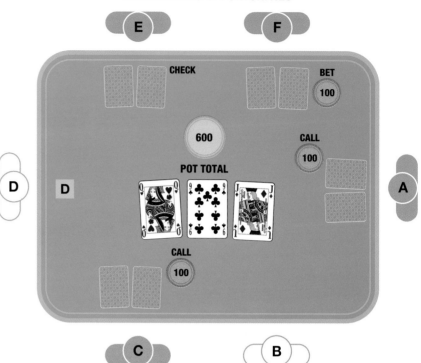

CHECKRAISING OPPORTUNITIES

PLAYER E

Above: By checking in early position after the flop, player E with a K-high straight has induced a bet and two calls from opponents and can now consider a raise with what is currently the best possible hand. Should everyone then fold, the manoeuvre will have successfully obtained a few more chips than might have been the case if player E had bet in turn. Alternatively, anyone who subsequently calls the raise will still be trailing and will need further help from the board, leaving player E in a strong position to manage the pot. The checkraise can also be a viable bluffing tactic if the board cards offer the credible threat of a made hand.

Checkraising

While many players deem checkraising, or 'sandbagging' – the latter a tactic of slow-playing a strong hand, perhaps by checkraising – to be an underhand ploy, the fact remains that it is a perfectly legitimate ploy in a game premised, after all, on deception. As an aid to pot management, it allows a player who holds a strong hand in an early position to lure opponents into betting more than intended. Should a check be followed by a bet and a couple of calls from others at the table, a raise might be enough to win straight away. At the very least it might persuade one or two opponents to fold, thus reducing the field and leaving the checkraiser in good shape for the turn, with probably the best hand.

In pot-limit and no-limit Texas Hold 'em, the checkraise is a more powerful bluffing tool than in the fixed-limit game, but players have to be sure that conditions are right. The potential offered by the flop must act as a guide, for it is the board cards that a player must use to engender fear in opponents. For instance, players in late positions will frequently try to pick up the pot if the action has been checked to them, even with a modest hand. If the flop suggests the potential for a much better hand to exist, a checkraise in early position may be sufficient to convince opponents that it is already held. A flop of Qs, 9h, 8c, for example, would make a straight for someone holding J, 10 but, if the betting is checked around, anyone holding a hand such as A, Q or A, 9 may bet in the belief they are leading. By checking and then raising with a large bet to imply possession of the straight, opponents with such hands are instantly put onto the back foot. Even if the bluff is called, any K, J or 10 on the turn followed by a large bet can reinforce belief in the opponents' minds that the straight has definitely been achieved.

SLOW-PLAYING A HAND

PLAYER F

Above: Deceiving opponents is an essential element of Texas Hold 'em, so being able to disguise the strength of a hand is a tactical move that can pay dividends. In this example, player F resisted the urge to raise before the flop with the pair of kings and has generated a family pot in which everybody remains involved. By checking on the flop, the hope is that others will sense weakness and bet with hands far inferior to the trip kings. Slow-playing the hand in this fashion, therefore, is a tactic that can increase its profitability as opponents inflate the pot with little or no chance of winning.

Left: A pocket pair of jacks which is best regarded as a medium pair only. Notoriously tricky to play, pocket jacks can be played aggressively from late position if nobody is keen to raise the pot. Calling with a pair of jacks when an opponent has already raised is much more testing, though, since any A, K or Q on the flop will often have made a higher pair.

SLOW-PLAYING A HAND
♦ ♣ ♥ ♠

When holding an exceptionally strong hand on the flop, players are best advised to slow-play it by simply checking or calling as needed to keep opponents involved. A flop of Kh, 6d, 4c when holding pocket kings, for example, is unlikely to have helped many opponents given that the cards needed for a straight draw are so low. Here, the player with trip kings can probably allow opponents to see the turn card cheaply and reserve bigger bets for the last two betting rounds. While an opponent may strike lucky, there remains a 30 per cent chance that the trip kings could still improve to a full house or four of a kind, which would be highly unlikely to lose.

The turn

The revealing of the turn card, or 'fourth street' as it sometimes known, clarifies the situation even more, as players face the same considerations as on the flop. The difference lies in the fact that with just one card to come, assessing one's own hand and comparing it with the best that might result on the river, the last card, is much simpler.

Equally, calculating the pot odds when considering whether to bet or not is a straightforward task. Crucially, it must be remembered that any card that helps one player may improve an opponent's hand as well. The danger in this situation is that, having survived as far as the turn card, it is very easy to become committed to the pot and see the hand through to the showdown. Despite believing it is a probable loser, the amount in the pot and the proximity to claiming it can all too easily prompt a player into casting good money after bad.

Playing the turn

As ever, discipline and realism are needed at this point in the game, irrespective of how many chips a player has already contributed to the pot. The fact that the minimum bet on the turn and the river is double that of the previous two rounds should encourage players to be circumspect regarding their chances.

Once again, how to play the turn is dependent on a player's position, the number of opponents and the betting that has already occurred. A maximum bet when clearly leading is advisable, to put pressure on opponents with drawing hands who, although tempted by the pot odds on offer, will need to improve on the river to win. In most cases, some doubt will remain over the ultimate result. For instance, if a flop of 4h, Ac, Jh is supplemented with the 6h on the turn, then a player holding Ah, Js is in a reasonable position with the

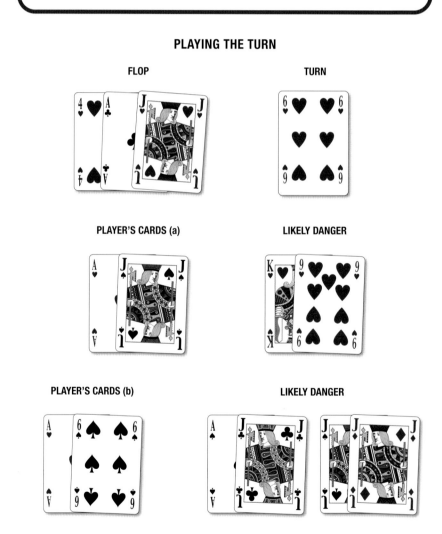

PLAYING THE TURN

FLOP	TURN
PLAYER'S CARDS (a)	LIKELY DANGER
PLAYER'S CARDS (b)	LIKELY DANGER

Above: The quality of a hand depends on the flop, but doubt over the final outcome can still exist once the turn card is revealed. The A, J offsuit for the top two pairs and the nut flush draw is still vulnerable if a bet on the flop is called, indicating that an opponent may have two hearts. The possibility of a flush draw having been made on the turn is high, but the player holding A, J still has 11 cards that can win, with the aces, jacks and remaining hearts all helping.

top two pairs and odds of about 3 to 1 against making the nut flush or a full house. Only an opponent who has already made a flush – which could yet be beaten – is likely to call, or more likely raise, any bet in this situation.

By contrast, if the player holds Ah, 6s instead, given the same board cards, then the options are less promising, especially if the betting on the flop indicated that one opponent may also have an A while another was drawing to the flush. Now only another heart on the river can guarantee success, since an A, 6 or a J could give an opponent a better full house. Therefore, choosing whether to bet in this situation must be guided by the inferences drawn from earlier play.

Reading the betting

While players are naturally inclined to focus on their own prospects of winning, the clues on offer from the betting of opponents are ignored only by the foolhardy. Whatever the standard of the game, players bet for a reason and deducing the rationale behind their strategy is all part of the challenge presented by Texas Hold 'em. For example if a flop of 10s, 2c, 5c generated only light betting, but a player in early position bets after the turn card is revealed as the 4c, then a flush is surely indicated.

Should that player hold Ac, Jc for the nut flush and be raised by an opponent, then the natural conclusion, however unlikely, is that a straight flush has been secured with pocket cards of 6c, 3c. An opponent with a lower-ranking flush may have called, but would probably credit the player with possession of the Ac for a flush draw at least, making the hand vulnerable.

Any player trying to draw to the flush without the Ac, meanwhile, is likely to fold. The danger for the player

Above: A sizeable pot develops as the game unfolds. In a fairly loose Texas Hold 'em game that features several players regularly paying to see the turn card, substantial pots can develop. As the minimum bet doubles after the turn, players must be certain in their own minds that contributing more chips to the pot is justified by the strength of their cards, not merely the size of the pot on offer.

READING THE BETTING

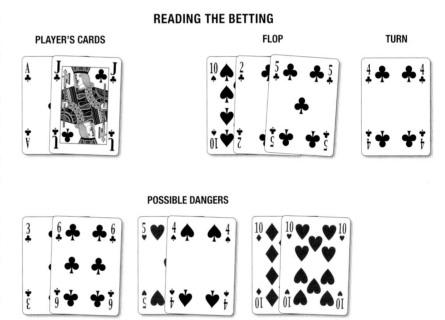

Above: Clues to the strength of an opponent's hand will usually arise from the betting and, on occasions, players have to accept that the improbable can happen. A player holding Ac, Jc, for example, would normally expect to take the pot if a third club should appear on the turn. But if the betting up to this point has been light, players with weak starting hands could still be in contention. Should a bet supporting the A-high flush be called, it is possible that an opponent could be drawing to a full house. However, a raise from an opponent would logically indicate that an unlikely straight flush has been achieved with the 3c, 6c.

with the Ac, Jc in this example comes from calling the raise while potentially already losing, only to see the 3c, 6c, 7c or 8c on the river. Judging by the betting, a straight flush for the opponent would then seem highly likely, not just possible.

The river

Typically, it is rare for more than three players to be contesting the pot by the time the river card is dealt, whichever betting structure is in place. Players should expect that anyone still in opposition at this stage must like something about the board cards, even if to win they may yet need to execute an impressive bluff.

Once the final card is revealed, players are able to see exactly what their hand comprises and also the potential hands available to opponents. Yet the best hand may still not win depending on the perceived threats held by the board cards and the nature of the betting throughout play. Unless holding the nuts, calling a large bet with a hand that is a potential but not guaranteed winner can test the nerves of even the most experienced player. Whether such a call would be justified depends on the likelihood of the hand proving the best and, as usual, whether the pot odds favour a call even if it is likely to lose. Clues are available from the cards and the previous betting rounds, and play on the river often hinges upon a correct reading of the game. In this regard, knowledge of opponents' playing styles is often crucial, although sitting in on a game with total strangers, as when playing online, understandably makes this more difficult.

Available options

There are not too many options available on the river. A player holding what seems to be a winning hand must concentrate on pot management by doing what it takes to encourage opponents to contribute more chips. In early position during a pot-limit or no-limit game, a small bet relative to those of previous rounds might be enough to goad an opponent into calling, just to prove that the hand represented is actually held.

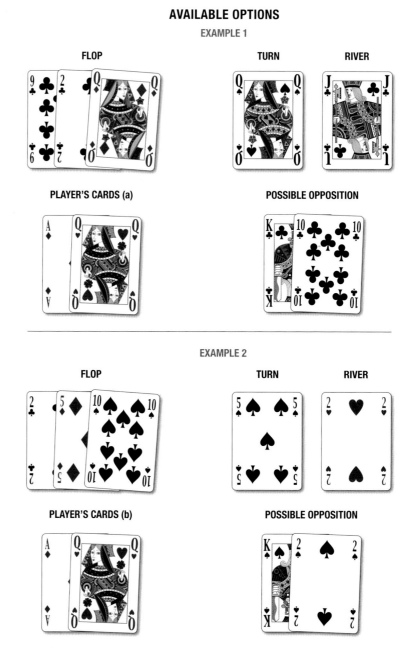

AVAILABLE OPTIONS

EXAMPLE 1

FLOP   TURN   RIVER

PLAYER'S CARDS (a)   POSSIBLE OPPOSITION

EXAMPLE 2

FLOP   TURN   RIVER

PLAYER'S CARDS (b)   POSSIBLE OPPOSITION

Above: Clues from the previous betting rounds will help to make a decision on the river, especially when a strong hand may have been beaten on the river. In example 1, the player holding three queens would have to fear that an opponent had completed a flush if the opponent had previously called a large bet after the turn card. In example 2, holding the A in a light betting heat may be enough to win when the board reveals two low pairs and a medium kicker. But a lack of earlier betting action may ensure the final round is contested by several players, any of which could hold a vital low card such as a 2 to make an unlikely full house.

FISH, GEESE AND SHEEP
♦ ♣ ♥ ♠

Those unable to read a game are considered weak players with 'fish', 'geese' and 'sheep' being just a few of the common terms used by experienced players to refer to them. The challenge for novices is to improve with experience, to avoid continually making the right move at the wrong time. Competent amateur players may be regarded as 'fish' when they move up to a higher level and start competing with the sharks of the professional poker world.

JUDGEMENT CALLS
♦ ♣ ♥ ♠

Playing the river when not holding the best possible hand is a common experience for all Texas Hold 'em players, although this is often due to the inclination of many to keep calling bets from the flop onwards with hands that improve just enough to put them in further trouble. A player holding Ad, 3d, for instance, may have stayed to the end, having seen the board cards revealed as As, 8s, Kh, 6c and finally 3s. But if an opponent has matched bets all the way, it is unsafe to assume that two pairs of aces and threes will be enough to win. If the betting has been at the minimum level throughout, then the opponent probably has an A, could already have two higher pairs and might conceivably have played for the flush draw holding Ks, Qs. Sometimes, however, the river card may simply complete a nondescript board, which makes it possible for a player with, perhaps, just an A-high, to steal the pot by betting first. Judging whether to try this move will depend on how confident a player is that small bets and checks in previous rounds confirm that nobody has a hand good enough to call such a bet.

A bet is advised in a fixed-limit game, as there is no point in allowing opponents to check and thus miss the chance of winning a few more chips.

When in a later position, playing the leading hand is more straightforward, since a bet or raise can always be made in confidence. Hands that are made on or before the river but could easily be beaten are more difficult to play. Having three of a kind by the turn when the river card puts a third club on the board, for example, is an awkward position to be in if it is plausible an opponent has pursued the flush all along.

Similarly, a board of two pairs and a low kicker will sometimes generate little action and be won by a player holding an A. It is difficult to call a large bet with the highest kicker when the prospect of encountering a slow-played full house looms. Players will then sometimes have to rely on their instincts concerning the opposition as much as the odds at work.

The river card will often signal the failure of some players to draw the card needed for a straight or a flush. Folding is the usual option here, unless the board holds the promise of a bluff. These are more likely to succeed in games that permit large bets, since, in fixed-limit Texas Hold 'em, the cost of calling is simply not enough to force opponents to surrender the chips already bet.

Left: Once the river card has been dealt to the board, a player who holds the nuts should definitely bet, the real test being to stake just enough that opponents with inferior hands are tempted to call for fear of being bluffed. If the bet is too big, the opposition may well fold leaving the winner of the hand with a smaller profit than might have been the case.

JUDGEMENT CALLS

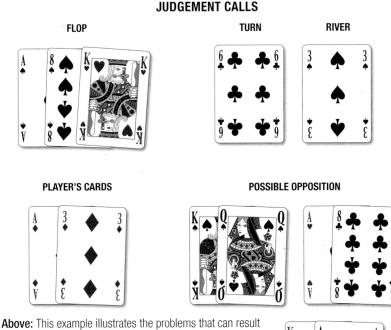

FLOP | **TURN** | **RIVER**

PLAYER'S CARDS | **POSSIBLE OPPOSITION**

Above: This example illustrates the problems that can result by the river when playing an A with a low kicker. The A on the flop for a high pair offered promise, but if any bet on the flop or the turn was called, then any one of several credible hands could be in opposition. An opponent with an A and a higher kicker could easily have made two better pairs, while a flush is equally possible. In this instance, the improvement for the A, 3 could lead to a player calling a bet with a beaten hand.

Know your opponents

Successful Texas Hold 'em players are obviously aware of the opportunities presented by various starting hands and the board cards as they are revealed. What separates the excellent players from those of average ability, however, is their aptitude for quickly gauging an opponent's playing style and reacting accordingly. Indeed, the very best players will alternate their style throughout a session to confuse and unsettle opponents, many of whom are prone to make predictable moves governed by their personality. Such players generally fall into one of four recognizable categories, irrespective of the stake level at which they normally play poker.

Know your solid players

Solid players, often known as 'rocks', are those who have the discipline and patience to fold the majority of hands and cautiously wait for an unbeatable hand – the nuts – or something very close to it, before committing too many chips to the pot. Conscious of their playing position at all times and the chip stacks in front of their opponents, they have a tendency to play only the highest-ranking starting hands and support them vigorously unless there are enough loose players at the table to justify setting a trap. In fixed-limit games, such players will play the percentages and seize upon mistakes.

Know your tight-aggressive players

At high-stakes tournament level, most solid players will adopt a tight-aggressive mode of play, folding anything but the best starting hands and pressurizing opponents with large pre-flop raises that leave little doubt as to the strength of their pocket cards. On those occasions when their strategy backfires, however, such players will still retain the discipline to fold rather than chase their losses.

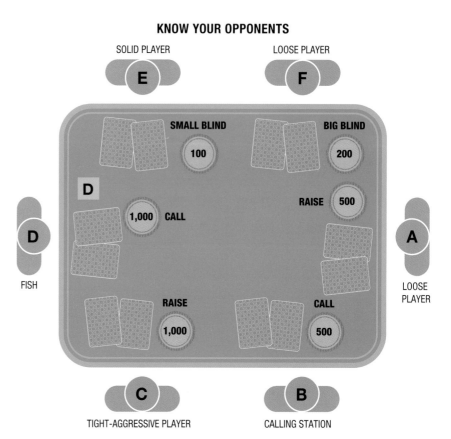

KNOW YOUR OPPONENTS

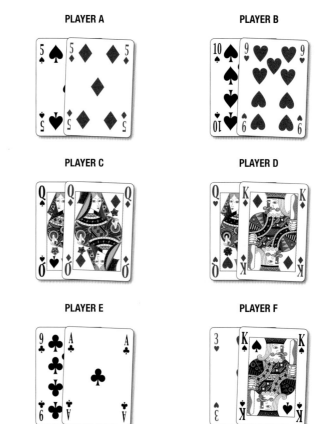

Above: Each individual's style of play has a bearing on any game. After the deal in this no-limit Texas Hold 'em contest, player A raises out of position with a low pair, in keeping with an enterprising approach, while player B cannot resist calling, due to a desire to be in the action. Player C, with a strong hand, takes advantage by raising again with the pair of queens, only to be called by inexperienced player D, who is unable to read the implications of previous bets. The solid player E will be prepared to fold the A, 9 suited for the loss of the small blind, but a loose player on the big blind could call the further 800 chips for the remote chance of winning.

Know your loose players

Those who play poker for social rather than financial reasons are likely to indulge in a much looser style of play. A desire to stay in the action characterizes such players, and their enthusiasm for Texas Hold 'em will make them likely to call a raise when holding a small pair or 8, 7 suited in the small blind, for example, after which they may disregard the pot odds for an outside chance of winning.

Other examples of loose play include raising repeatedly when out of position and calling in contradiction of the evidence on display when needing cards to win. Such players tend to have volatile periods of good and bad fortune, and their hands are difficult to read, making them dangerous opponents.

Know your calling stations

For a player with pretensions to winning, knowing the 'calling stations' – these being players who repeatedly call other players' bets, irrespective of their chances of winning – is crucial. These players will frequently upset the odds by drawing unlikely winning hands. Being suspicious by nature, they find it difficult to release any chance of winning a pot, even in the face of particularly antagonistic betting. No matter how big the raise or how unlikely their chances of winning, calling stations will play sheriff as they insist on verifying that the raiser has the hand being represented.

The tendency to call, irrespective of the pot odds or inferences on offer during play, is very common among novices. They are often insufficiently familiar with the nuances of the game to understand the inferences behind a bet, which makes them very difficult to bluff. Should a good player not realize soon enough that an opponent is unable to interpret the meaning behind large bets, valuable chips could quickly change ownership when bluffs are repeatedly called.

IMPACT ON THE BETTING

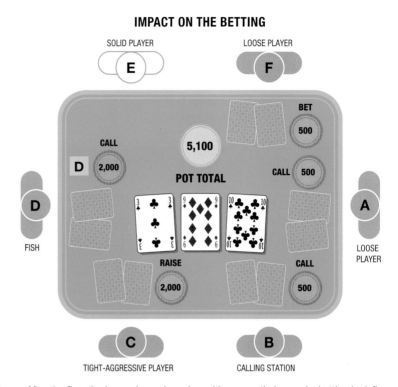

Above: After the flop, the loose players in early position press their case by betting in defiance of the pre-flop raise by player C who again tries to force the opposition out of the pot. However, player D sees a possible straight materializing and calls another big raise, unaware that the pot odds are vastly inferior to the chances of catching a J, one of which – Jc – could make someone else a flush. With over 10,000 chips in the pot, players F, A and B may yet contribute more, as the potential rewards for winning override their concerns at being beaten.

SAME HANDS, DIFFERENT APPROACH

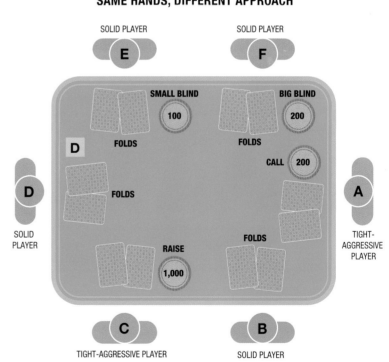

Above: By way of contrast with the first two examples, here the same pre-flop situation is replicated, but in a game between solid and experienced players. A flat call from player A with the low pair is raised by player C, who, content to pick up the pot right now, presses home the early advantage with the pair of queens. Player D reads this as indicative of a high pair and knows that if player C has kings or queens, then chances of improvement are low. Player E will fear that player C has an A with a bigger kicker, undermining the A, 9 suited. Both players fold, as does player F, so player A faces a hard call for 800 chips with a hand that should probably be folded.

Betting structures

Although much of the expert guidance available on how to play Texas Hold 'em is relevant, whichever betting structure is in place, each has sufficient impact on the culture of the game to warrant consideration. The stakes are important too, emphasizing that anyone buying in to a game ought to play at a stake level commensurate with their financial means. Players who participate in games for money that they cannot afford to lose are rarely able to focus entirely on their poker and run the risk of compounding their error with poor play. Contrasting betting structures were devised to satisfy the tastes of different players and their various gambling preferences, with three in particular emerging as the most popular.

Fixed-limit

This is the betting structure favoured by the majority of recreational cash game players, although there are numerous professionals who grind out a living playing fixed-limit Texas Hold 'em in the casinos and card rooms of the world. In the resort casinos of Las Vegas and Atlantic City, the small-stakes limit games are frequently populated by 'rounders' – itinerant gamblers who play only premium hands and sit patiently waiting for the tourists to make mistakes.

Therein lies a clue as to the best way to play fixed-limit Texas Hold 'em, which is a game of position, and percentages. It favours conservative players who are reluctant to gamble wildly, since the scale of any betting during a hand is easier to predict. This helps players to calculate the upper limit of any possible losses while devising their betting strategy.

Right: In no-limit Texas Hold 'em the daunting prospect of throwing away all of one's chips in a single hand is always present.

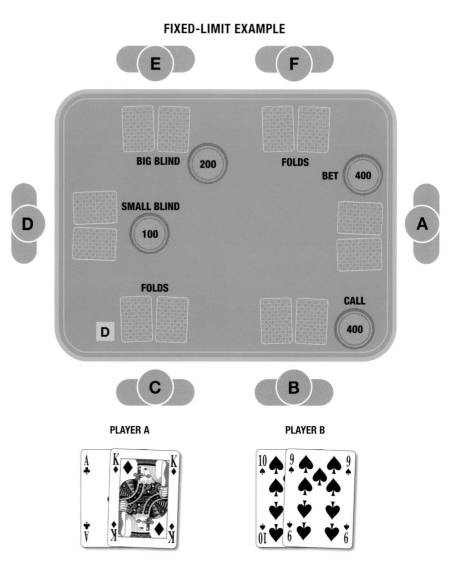

FIXED-LIMIT EXAMPLE

Above: Raising before the flop with A, K offsuit is a perfectly legitimate tactic, whichever betting structure is in place, but the difficulties of pressing home the advantage in a fixed-limit game are illustrated here. Player B only has to call twice the minimum bet to stay in the game, while those players in the blinds could well call, even with mediocre hands, to see if the flop brings any help. Player A's attempt to reduce the field to perhaps one opponent, over whom the A, K will probably be a favourite to win, is thus hampered by the limit on the size of raise permitted.

In general, players are advised to apply rigid standards to the quality of hands they play, relative to their betting position. Pre-flop raises are less common in this form of the game, since it is difficult to force up to nine opponents to fold for the cost of a single bet. Following the flop, a checkraise in early position may suggest enough threat to cause opponents to fold, but bluffing in this position is rather hazardous. Indeed, bluffing is best kept to a minimum, as players are restricted from betting the sums needed to intimidate the opposition.

Pot-limit

Popular with both professionals and amateurs, pot-limit Texas Hold 'em allows the freedom for players to bet more aggressively in support of their strong hands, to reduce the opposition and improve their chances of winning. Pots can quickly escalate in size, but a typical game with blinds set at a nominal level often features several players willing to see the flop. Making a pre-flop raise may encourage some opponents to fold, but the serious action normally begins after the flop has been revealed, since this is when most players are able to define their chances. If they are good, then the betting can be expected to increase, although it may not be until the turn card is dealt that the pot-sized bets start to appear.

So, while the cost of seeing the flop may be relatively small, players are often happy to call with modest hands because the prospect of picking up a very large pot when the flop fits is that much greater than in the fixed-limit game.

Left: A player bets all-in before the flop having decided that, with just a few chips remaining, the hole cards justify taking the risk. Most often seen in no-limit games where making an all-in bet can be an aggressive tactic, players may still find themselves going all-in during fixed-limit games when they have fewer chips than required to make the minimum bet.

NO-LIMIT EXAMPLE

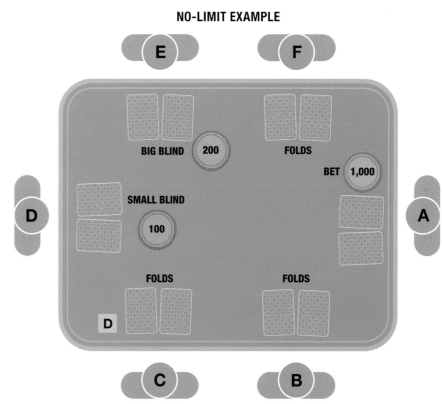

Above: By way of contrast, when there is no limit on the maximum bet, player A is better able to represent strength in an effort to dissuade opponents from calling. Player B's 10, 9 suited may have been worth a call of 400 chips in the fixed-limit example, but calling a pre-flop bet of 1,000 chips is much more difficult with the same hand. Unless the players in the blinds have at least a medium pair, they will probably surrender the pot, enabling player A to pick up the blinds with this aggressive move.

PLAYER B

NO-LIMIT TEXAS HOLD 'EM
♦ ♣ ♥ ♠

No-limit Texas Hold 'em is the most prominent of all tournament poker games and is regarded by many professionals as the most challenging variation currently being played. While it obviously suits the tournament format, the fact that players only ever stand to lose what may be a modest entry fee can disguise the inherent difficulties of playing it well as a cash game. For anyone hoping to make a modest bankroll stretch over several hours, buying in to a no-limit Texas Hold 'em game promises only anxiety and tension when an entire stack of chips could be lost in one hand. A tight or aggressive style is regarded as the most effective in the long term, which requires folding the majority of hands and betting aggressively, perhaps with a pre-flop raise, when holding premium cards. Having the patience to withstand such aggression from opponents while hoping to see cheap flops and light betting could lead to plenty of inactivity. Yet aggression is definitely an asset in the no-limit game, meaning that anyone who is not prepared to risk their entire chip stack on one hand is probably better suited to fixed-limit Texas Hold 'em.

Tournament play

Prior to the inception of the WSOP in 1970, tournament poker was virtually unknown, but this situation has changed dramatically. The success of the knockout format and the concept of the winner taking all permeated Las Vegas casinos and soon spread to the rest of the world. By the end of the 20th century, television had realized the potential for tournament poker to offer keen entertainment. No-limit Texas Hold 'em has since emerged as the most widespread tournament game, but fixed-limit and pot-limit Texas Hold 'em tournaments are also a key part of the professional circuit, as well as being popular in poker rooms, both real and online.

A new challenge

Although the basic concepts behind sound Texas Hold 'em play are relevant to tournaments, players must adjust their strategic thinking, to take account of the different context. The search for a definitive winner and the systematic increases in the blinds force players into taking a few more risks than might be the case in a cash game. The ebbs and flows of competition, and the corresponding impact on a player's chip stack, trigger many decisive confrontations as competitors try to keep themselves in contention for a share of the prize money.

Critics consider that luck plays too big a part in tournament poker and that the public's affection for knockout games owes much to a desire for quick and decisive results. For cash game devotees who take a long-term view of their work, constantly raising the blinds in order to provoke the inevitable confrontations is anathema, because hands that would ordinarily be folded, frequently have to be played during a tournament. Some players are highly skilled at both forms of the game, and there are enough successful tournament professionals who consistently finish in the money to suggest that, at the highest level at least, luck remains no substitute for skill and experience.

Choosing a tournament

The phenomenal success of world-class tournaments, is partly because anyone who wishes to enter usually has only to pay the required entry fee. This could run into thousands of dollars since many of the events cost upwards of US$1,000, with the fee for entering the WSOP world championship game currently set at US$10,000. That does not prevent the tournament from attracting up to 8,000 players for a competition that takes the best part of a week to complete.

TYPICAL TOURNAMENT SET-UP

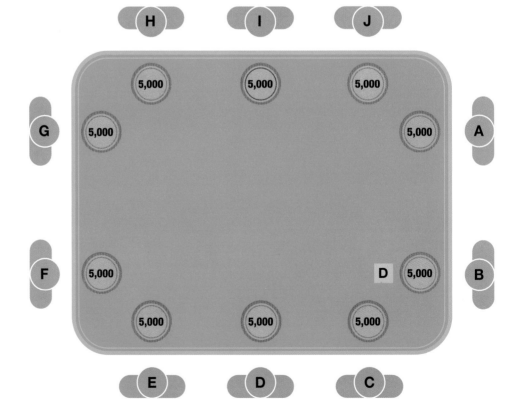

Right: This represents the typical scene at the beginning of a tournament, with up to ten players seated at the table and each starting with, in this case, 5,000 chips. A single-table tournament would feature a maximum of ten players, but a multi-table tournament featuring one hundred entrants would see this scene replicated on nine other tables as play commences. The dealer button (D), which is moved clockwise round the table after each deal, indicates that player B will be the nominal dealer for the first hand. Card rooms will often employ a professional dealer to conduct proceedings, leaving the players free to concentrate on play.

PRIZE STRUCTURES
♦ ♣ ♥ ♠

The prize structure in the formative years of tournament play was often a simple case of the winner taking all. Gradually, as tournament poker grew in popularity, the prize pools on offer led to a more equitable distribution of cash prizes, with the top 10 per cent of entrants now likely to win sufficient to cover their entry fee at least. To claim the more substantial prizes, however, still requires a player to finish in the top three or four per cent which is, understandably, a major challenge. The breakdown of the prize pool varies according to the numbers involved, the winner often claiming 50 per cent in events comprising less than 50 players, but only 25 per cent in those featuring 200 players or more. Although obviously more difficult to win, it is the prospect of turning a few dollars into a few thousand that makes large-scale, multi-table tournaments so appealing.

At a lower level, regular tournaments for players with tighter budgets exist, with online poker rooms offering the tournament experience for pocket-money entrance fees. The tournaments are varied in terms of style and structure. Daily or weekly competitions in real and online card rooms are supplemented by sit 'n' go tournaments, satellites, freerolls, qualifiers, turbo tournaments and single-table or multi-table events. There are also freeze-out or rebuy tournaments, meaning that, in terms of consumer choice, there is likely to be a tournament structure to suit every Texas Hold 'em player. Deciding which one to play will depend on a player's own personal tastes and financial means.

Above: A stack of chips as used in the European Poker Championships. Specifically branded chips are common in casinos and the idea extends to tournament events as well. Apart from the obvious promotional aspects associated with such branding, there is a practical purpose behind the use of exclusive chips since it prevents players from introducing chips from one establishment into a game at another.

Left: Joe Hachem from Melbourne, Australia, kisses a stack of US$100 bills having won the first prize of US$7.5 million at the WSOP world championship in 2005. Entries for the event have increased massively over the last decade, fuelled by thousands of online qualifiers, leading to a corresponding increase in the top prize. The US clampdown on online gaming in late 2006 led to a small reduction in entries for the WSOP world championship games of 2007 and 2008.

Early stages

Since no-limit Texas Hold 'em is the most popular tournament game, the general considerations detailed here will focus on the situations encountered in such an event, although many of the comments will apply equally well to pot-limit and fixed-limit contests. Also, any reference to cash sums will be in US dollars, this being the common currency of poker the world over.

The entry fees involved have an impact, with it being likely that players will play more loosely in a freeroll tournament in which there is no entry fee at all than they would having paid US$1,000 for the privilege of competing. In a similar vein, tournaments that offer the chance to rebuy chips during the first hour or two of play also invite players to take chances early on in the game. A successful all-in bet could double or triple a player's chip stack to secure an advantage, which is a tempting move, given that immediate elimination from the tournament is not at stake.

Freeze-out tournaments, the main focus of attention here, are generally characterized by most players easing themselves into the game as they assess their opponents. However, even these will include a minority of players who play aggressively from the start.

Stealing the blinds

The difference between cash games and tournaments is that the blinds will rise at specified intervals of anything between two minutes and a couple of hours. Players who sit waiting for a perfect hand to materialize risk being anted away before having a chance to act. Irrespective of whether playing in a single or multi-table tournament, the need to put in the occasional pre-flop raise to steal the blinds must be considered. Successful moves such as this, whether they are bluffs or not, help to keep a player's chip stack intact while covering the cost of the compulsory bets as the deal moves round the table.

While the blinds are modest at the start, the need to pressurize the blinds when there is little interest before the flop is a recurring theme during play as they increase in scale. Since this tactic is common, combating such a move when in the big blind, for example, usually needs possession of a good starting hand to justify a call. If one opponent repeatedly targets a specific player in this situation, a substantial re-raise might put them off doing so for a while. In tournament play, timing is everything, since one wrong move can devastate a player's chip stack, if not guarantee elimination.

Right: This shows the situation in a typical tournament after the betting has already risen through a couple of levels. The total number of chips currently held by each player is indicated, all having started the tournament with 5,000 chips. The player in seat D has been eliminated, with player E having profited from the early action. Player C is under the most pressure, because, with the blinds having risen from 25 (small) and 50 (big) to 100 and 200, for example, the minimum bet represents more than one-twelfth of the player's total chip count. As players are eliminated during a multi-table tournament, others are moved from adjoining tables to occupy vacated seats. This keeps the ratio of players per table consistent and enables the organizers to gradually reduce the number of tables in operation.

EARLY STAGES

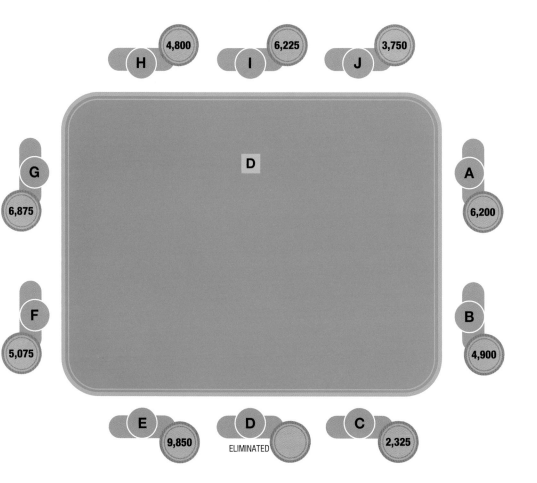

Survival of the fittest

At the beginning of a tournament, each player receives an equal number of chips, the objective being to amass the total in play by eliminating all opposition. Events in which the blind levels are raised every 15 minutes or less do not provide much scope for players to remain patient. However, while some aggression is required, players should still be wary of fighting early betting wars when dealt only fair starting hands. Those who are intent on pursuing a death-or-glory policy can usually be left to eliminate each other as the tournament settles into its rhythm.

No tournament is ever won within the first few hands, so surviving until the later stages of the game should be uppermost in players' minds. This is certainly true in events with much longer intervals between the increased betting levels. The general advice is for players to monitor the level of the average chip stack and stay ahead of that figure. In online tournaments, such information is updated after each hand, but at a multi-table event in a real card room, a quick glance at the other tables for an assessment of the opposition's chip standing might be necessary. There is no suggestion that a player holding a premium hand should never consider betting aggressively. Good opportunities to double-up with an all-in bet will occur, but only by exercising a high degree of selectivity over which hands to play – and when – will a player maintain interest in a competition.

Above: Jeff Williams, the American student who won the 2006 EPT Grand Final in Monte Carlo having qualified via satellite tournaments on the PokerStars online site. Though experienced tournament professionals often have the edge in big events, the proliferation of online poker tournaments means that Internet players can rapidly develop the skills required.

STEALING THE BLINDS

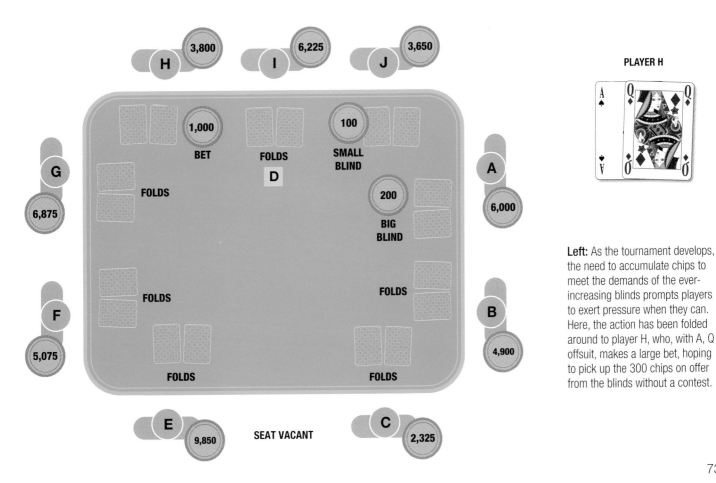

PLAYER H

Left: As the tournament develops, the need to accumulate chips to meet the demands of the ever-increasing blinds prompts players to exert pressure when they can. Here, the action has been folded around to player H, who, with A, Q offsuit, makes a large bet, hoping to pick up the 300 chips on offer from the blinds without a contest.

Middle stages

As the tournament nears its middle stages, with as many as half the original starters already eliminated, the strategy to adopt very much depends on how many chips a player still holds. Being the chip leader is obviously beneficial, but holding a better-than-average chip position should at least help a player fend off the pressure of the ever-increasing blinds.

By now, the big blind could easily be as much as a fifth of the original starting stack, emphasizing the need to keep picking up pots on a regular basis. A run of poor cards in the face of aggressive betting can make this prospect exceedingly difficult, so making a few bluffs is almost unavoidable.

Under normal circumstances, many of the loose and reckless players will have been knocked out by this stage. As a result, the more astute players who are left may be more susceptible to a credible bluff, since they have a sharper awareness of the inferences behind any bet. Also, as the possibility of claiming a prize draws closer for those managing to avoid elimination, players are sometimes prone to becoming more defensive, which presents another situation to be exploited.

Chip count

From the middle stages onwards, it becomes essential for players to monitor their opponents' chip positions as well as their own. Assuming that to finish in the prizes means making the final table, a keen eye on the chip counts will help guide a player's tactical and strategic thinking as the number of opponents dwindles. Anyone in the top third has the chance to fold a succession of hands and avoid confrontations, while short-stacked opponents battle against each other. Also, the possibility of intimidating opponents with the occasional large raise to force them all-in if they call is another available tactic.

Short-stacked players can expect to be pressurized all the time as the blinds eat into their reserves. In this position there may not be time to wait for a large

PLAYER A

Right: The ability to change gear during the middle stages of a tournament is a major asset. This means that players may start to bet with lower-ranking starting hands than usual when they have an above-average chip count and the advantage of position. For those low on chips, pressure will come from all quarters and they may have little option but to go all-in with a poor hand. Here, for example, player J makes a substantial raise that threatens each of those still to act with elimination in this hand, given that there are three further betting rounds to negotiate. Player B, in particular, has a limited number of opportunities to survive, given the big blind is approaching, but decides to fold the J, 8 offsuit on this occasion. The action now is on player D, who has an uncomfortable decision to make with the pair of sevens.

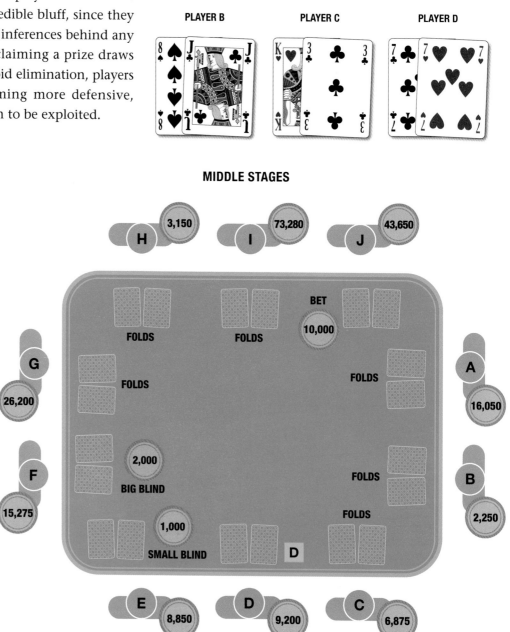

pair or A, K before pushing all the remaining chips into the pot, so opportunities with lesser hands have to be taken. Certainly, when a player is down to no more than five times the big blind, every hand must be considered in terms of its all-in potential, although the need to double-up one's stack may arise sooner than that. Another point to bear in mind is that the chip leaders may also fold in the face of aggression from mid-ranking players, since they could well be reluctant to sacrifice valuable chips with a place at the final table beckoning.

Changing gear

The ability to vary one's style of play is an asset in any form of poker, but being able to change gear during a tournament can help improve or stabilize a player's chip position. A burst of aggressive play featuring pre-flop and post-flop raises may be enough to win a few blinds and reluctant calls from opponents locked into a tight, conservative pattern. Winning enough to cover the blinds for another three or four circuits of the table will typically give a player 30 or more additional hands to consider and time to see more opponents eliminated.

This strategy is more effective when implemented by someone who has previously exhibited all the traits of a sound but cautious player. When short-stacked, such a ploy may smack of desperation, but for those within reach of the prize-money spots, it offers the chance to exploit any timidity in opponents, regardless of their chip position. It does mean being less selective over which starting hands to play, bringing with it the risk of being caught out by a strong hand. However, if the strategy is unsuccessful but still leaves a player with a manageable chip stack, consolidating for a while by reverting to caution once more remains an option.

As the tournament moves towards its conclusion, the value of a player's hole cards may be less significant to any betting strategy than the current chip positions of opponents. If three short-stacked opponents go all-in before the flop, even a large pair such as kings or aces may be worth folding. Competing against several opponents with a high pair simply increases the combined chances that one of them will beat the hand. Winning the pot could mean knocking out three opponents, but losing it could see just two of them eliminated, while the other emerges with a more substantial chip stack than need have been the case.

TACTICAL DECISIONS

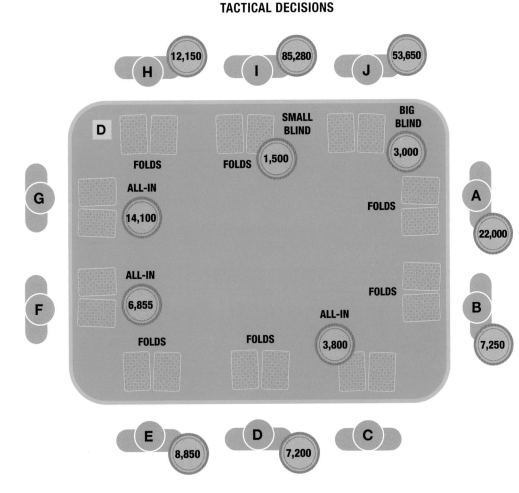

Left: As the pressure mounts, the need for discipline from those within touching distance of the final table increases. In this separate example, ordinarily player J would consider the pair of jacks worthy of a bet and, having already bet 3,000 chips in the big blind, a further bet of 11,100 to call player G could establish a chance to knock out three players in one hand. But a win for player G would see the pair of them in a similar chip position. Under the circumstances, a fold may be better, since a win for player G would still leave that opponent trailing player J by over 20,000 chips, which remains a significant advantage. This highlights how the value of the cards themselves may become less important compared to the other strategic concerns that develop throughout the tournament.

The end game

To reach the final table in any regular multi-table tournament, a player is likely to have prospered on several different tables, for a number of hours, against up to nine opponents at a time. Despite the fact that luck may well have played a part at some stage of the competition, it is the players with the skill to capitalize upon their fortune rather than relying on luck alone who will usually reach the prize-money spots. The difference between first place and tenth, however, will still be represented by a huge variation in the prizes available. Having successfully made it to the final table, plotting a strategy towards ultimate victory will again be dependent on the chips at a player's disposal.

Players who have short stacks will be highly aware that every hand could be their last and should bet all-in while they have enough chips to make the risk worthwhile. By allowing the stack to dwindle, a player might be faced with having to win a succession of all-in bets to find a way back into the game and, since many such confrontations provide no better than an even-money chance of winning, achieving this is exceedingly difficult.

Changing fortunes

Players with medium-sized chip stacks still need to exercise caution as the tournament reaches its final stages. Should the chip leader start bullying opponents with aggressive raises, it is best to avoid confrontations for as long as possible in the hope that those with shorter stacks succumb to the pressure. Raising a bet from an opponent with many more chips can only be confidently considered while holding an excellent hand.

As the eliminations continue and the number of players falls to four or five, the increased blinds will circulate the table much quicker. Players in the blinds can expect opponents to try stealing them with ever-larger bets, although judging what cards they hold becomes more of a challenge. With fewer players, the value of the average winning hand decreases and more risks are therefore taken with marginal starting hands.

Large pots contested by two players will develop repeatedly and fortunes can change rapidly. Having half as many chips as the leader when in an all-in battle will see the players swap positions should the low stack triumph, underlining that a tournament is never won until the final opponent has been eliminated.

THE FINAL TABLE

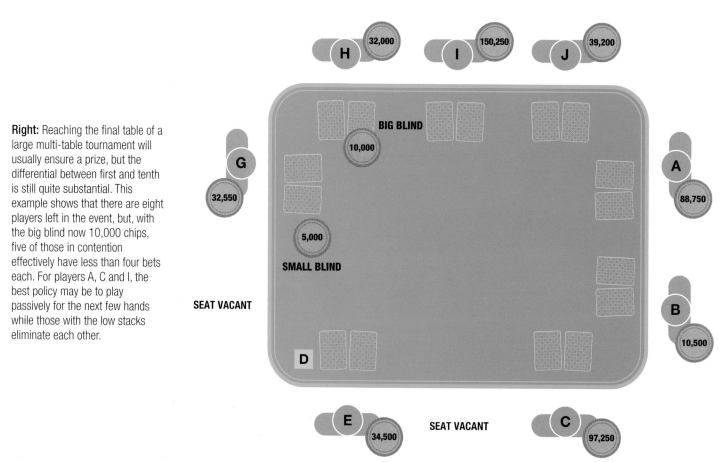

Right: Reaching the final table of a large multi-table tournament will usually ensure a prize, but the differential between first and tenth is still quite substantial. This example shows that there are eight players left in the event, but, with the big blind now 10,000 chips, five of those in contention effectively have less than four bets each. For players A, C and I, the best policy may be to play passively for the next few hands while those with the low stacks eliminate each other.

Heads-up

When there are only two players left competing heads-up at the table both will be assured of a prize usually well in excess of their entry fee. To secure victory, however, requires each player to pressurize the other with large bets, frequent bluffs and the willingness to support some weak starting hands.

Against one opponent, J, 7 offsuit represents the average hand and will win on half the occasions it is played. Holding a card higher than a J therefore offers a decent opportunity, while being dealt an A or any pair could easily warrant an all-in bet, whether having the majority or minority of chips.

Aggression is very important, since the blinds by this stage are usually so high that folding on two or three successive occasions can seriously weaken a player's chip position. Even when holding a substantial lead, with perhaps 80 per cent of the chips, a player cannot afford to fold too often, while losing to an all-in bet from an opponent on two successive occasions will see the lead change hands.

Generally, good heads-up play involves pressing home any perceived advantage as forcefully as possible in what amounts to an archetypal poker confrontation. Practising heads-up play is advisable, since there is no doubt that some players respond to the challenge of one-to-one combat much better than others. Ultimately, with almost every hand being contested, the conclusion to several hours of intense competition could be swift, with the winning hand often ranked lower than a pair. This may seem a little anti-climactic, given the quality of hands that will have been played to reach the last two, but both winner and runner-up will have successfully shown a consummate range of poker skills to be contesting the concluding hand of the tournament.

HEADS-UP

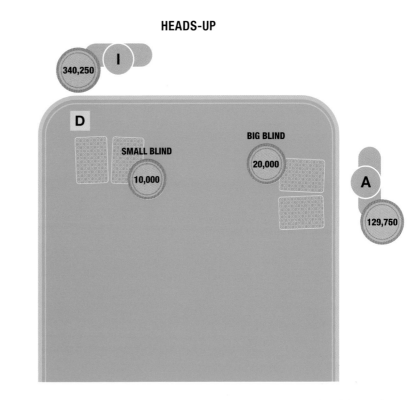

Above: When just two players are left, a heads-up situation exists, with the size of the blinds ensuring that almost every pot is worth contesting, irrespective of the cards held by each player. Ordinarily, a player either raises before the flop, or folds, since merely calling a bet invites an aggressive move from the opponent. This is the point at which a player's nerve is truly tested.

RAPIDLY CHANGING FORTUNES

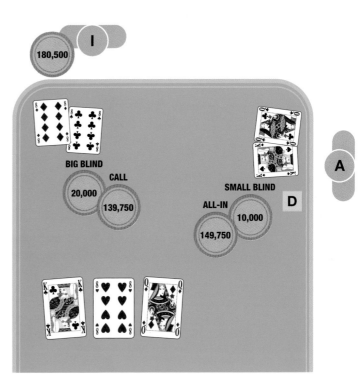

Above: Even a substantial chip lead at this stage of the game can soon be eradicated, with player I on the verge of winning here, having called player A's all-in bet from the small blind. Both have above-average hands and the flop, although favouring the chip leader, still provides player A with an outside chance to double up and take the lead. Any of the four remaining kings and queens in the deck will make a better full house and prompt another deal.

OMAHA

In Omaha, the action begins with the small blind and big blind being posted by the players to the dealer's left, just as in Texas Hold 'em. The dealer deals the cards one at a time to each player, clockwise around the table until everyone has four cards face down prior to the first betting round. Once the first-round betting is complete, the dealer reveals the flop which consists of three cards face up on the table which all players can use towards finalizing their hand. A second betting round takes place after which the turn card is dealt. Betting limits usually double at this stage of the game and, after a third betting round, the river card is revealed. This acts as a prelude to the final round of betting. The winner is the player who either makes an unmatched bet during the game or who holds the best poker hand at the showdown, of two hole cards and three from the board.

Below: When assessing which starting hands to play, consideration must be given to the likely possibilities presented by the board cards when they are all revealed. Half of the time, at least one pair will be present, as in the first example, making four of a kind a possibility and a full house almost certain. Players will usually need at least a straight to win and ample opportunities exist, since, as in the second example, three cards or more to a straight will appear on four out of every five occasions. However, flushes are regular winners, too, with three or more cards to a flush on the board occurring 40 per cent of the time as shown in the third example.

WHAT TO EXPECT FROM THE BOARD

FLOP	TURN	RIVER

EXAMPLE 1

EXAMPLE 2

EXAMPLE 3

Almost unheard of before the 1980s, Omaha – Omaha Hold 'em if preferred – is one of the most popular games played at home and online, and is firmly rooted on the professional circuit. Omaha tournaments reflect the most common betting structures applied to the game, though they are often played for high stakes. The pot-limit variation allows players room to manoeuvre, since the capacity to make pot-sized bets and raises creates bluffing opportunities. Fixed-limit Omaha tends to reward knowledgeable and often conservative players in the long run.

The game shares the same basic structure as Texas Hold 'em, with players receiving four hole cards, not two, prior to the five board cards being revealed. Also, their hands must comprise two hole cards and three from the board. These differences completely change the nature of the game and the strategies that should be applied in the search for success. The major factors to consider are reading the cards, understanding the odds and observing opponents. Acknowledging the impact of the betting structure – pot-limit or fixed-limit – on a player's strategic thinking is also important and this will be reflected in the following analysis of the game.

Crucial considerations

The starting point when considering any poker strategy is to contemplate the end of the game in order to understand the quality of hand that is likely to prevail. In draw poker or five-card stud, this may be as little as a pair of queens, while in Texas Hold 'em, two pairs and three of a kind are frequent winners. This is prone to confuse even experienced Texas Hold 'em players who are new to Omaha, a game in which a hand such as trip aces will very rarely prove good enough.

The minimum hand normally required to win at Omaha is a straight, but flushes and full houses are so frequent that even a straight is quite weak. Generally, it will win only when the board cards make a full house or flush impossible to achieve. Before assessing the relative merits of any starting hand, it is pertinent to consider the likely outcome on the board once the five community cards – the widow – have been revealed.

There are three key issues to remember, beginning with the fact that half the time at least one pair will appear, making a full house very likely. Second, at least

Above: Players receive four cards in Omaha prior to the first betting round and this represents a fairly good starting hand given that it comprises high-ranking cards and offers chances of a straight. It is, however, compromised by containing four hearts since this obviously reduces the number of available hearts in the deck with which the player could make a flush.

three cards of one suit will be seen in four out of every ten widows, emphasizing the potential for flushes. Third, 80 per cent of the time, three cards that fit a straight will be present, underlining why this is the minimum rank that hand players should be aiming to achieve.

Starting hands

Armed with a knowledge of what hands are likeliest to win at the showdown, players are better able to assess the quality of hand required to justify competing for the pot. After the deal, any four cards that offer realistic chances of full houses, flushes and straights are worth consideration, but Omaha is renowned as a game that is usually won by the best possible hand – the nuts. High-ranking cards, therefore, especially aces, have greater value because they offer players the chance to hit the best straights, flushes and full houses available. Given how often these hands occur, it is always preferable to have the nut flush when there is no pair on the board to indicate a full house might exist.

GOOD STARTING HANDS

Above: A good hand in Omaha is one in which all six two-card combinations offer a chance to fit the board cards to make a winning hand, with at least a straight required. High-ranking pocket cards are best, but their value is not as significant before the flop as in Texas Hold 'em. Both examples favour the highest-value straights, flushes and full houses and should be played.

FAIR STARTING HANDS

Above: Any hand that offers four or more viable combinations is certainly worthy of consideration. Here, the Ad, Qh, Qs, 7s offers full house and A-high straight possibilities, although the flush potential of the Qs, 7s combination is weak. Should the board feature three spades not including the A or K, then the Q-high flush is in danger of being outranked. The second example has fair straight and full house potential, but both the K, 8 combinations will need help from the board.

POOR STARTING HANDS

Above: Opening hands of low-ranking cards or less than three working combinations should be folded. A pair of nines may contribute to a full house, but it could be second-best, even if a 9 appears. To complete the full house would need a pair on the board and anything higher than a 9 – a pair of kings for example, will lose to anyone with a K and one other card matching the board. The straight potential of the 4, 3 combination is almost worthless, since a 5, 6, 7 on the board will lose to anyone holding 8, 4 or 9, 8. Similar problems apply to the other featured hand.

Good starting hands offer the most viable two-card combinations, of which there are six in all; the more of these that might fit any potential widow, the better the prospects of securing a playable hand. For instance, being dealt two pairs, such as Ad, As, 7h, 7c, is good, but holding Kd, Kc, Qd, Qc is arguably better. In the first case, the six combinations offer opportunities for a full house or even four of a kind, but the aces and sevens cannot be combined to make a straight. Having four different suits in the hand also rules out a flush. The second example, however, supplements the full house and four-of-a-kind potential, with the possibilities of high-ranking flushes and straights, offering more chances of success.

Pre-flop strategy

Before taking a closer look at the strategic possibilities that are presented by the first four cards, it is first worth highlighting other aspects of the game of Omaha that will have an influence on a player's betting decisions. In a high-stakes game featuring plenty of aggressive betting, players are far more likely to raise before the flop in an attempt to reduce the opposition. It is therefore a good policy to support only hands that offer multiple possibilities of winning. At a lower level, in fixed-limit home games, for example, pre-flop raises are much less likely, since the majority of players are inclined to call whatever cards are in their possession.

Essentially, this is what makes Omaha such a popular game, since social players enjoy the fact that even the most unpromising combination of hole cards will come good on the odd occasion. However, although players in a typical fixed-limit game will call to see perhaps half of all flops even with marginal hands, this does present them with the temptation of chasing hands that are destined to be second best. Pots can quickly escalate when there are several players involved, and this can encourage some of them to remain in the hand mistakenly pursuing value.

A constant appraisal of the odds and probabilities at work throughout the game remains the foundation for a disciplined approach to Omaha, and enables players to exploit those opponents who are always keen to be involved in the action.

Above: A player commits chips to the pot before the flop even though the hole cards displayed do not offer the greatest promise. Of the six two-card combinations available to the player, only two – the A, K and 6, 6 – have any merit in a hand that cannot make a flush because the cards are of four different suits. Unless the flop fits perfectly, the hand should probably be folded if an opponent bets in the second round.

Left: This example shows a strong starting hand which, because of the high value of the cards, has the potential to blend with a variety of flops to put the player in a good position. If the first three community cards are 9d, Ah, Qd then multiple opportunities open up for the player in the shape of straights, flushes and possibly even a full house.

Right: Irrespective of a starting hand, once the flop is dealt it is crucial to understand the implications behind the board cards, and identify what may form the nuts when all five are revealed. Anyone holding 9, 8 in the first example will have the best hand, with a straight, but a player with the A, K; A, Q or K, Q of clubs has the nut flush draw and the potential to hit a royal flush. The second example makes a full house probable and a player holding pocket kings will feel that kings over sixes will be enough, although the nuts at this stage is four sixes. Should nobody hold pocket sixes, then a further 6 on the board, or two aces, could yet see the hand beaten. Gauging the likelihood of that should always guide a player's betting strategy.

BE GUIDED BY THE FLOP

EXAMPLE 1

EXAMPLE 2

Seeking the nuts

The safest policy when contemplating Omaha is to remember that, once all the board cards have been shown, the winner in any showdown is likely to possess the nuts. This will not always be the case, but it should be at the forefront of any player's mind when holding a strong but not unbeatable hand and it should also be the guiding principle when assessing the options presented after the deal.

A good hand is one where the first four cards combine to offer six viable two-card hands. Having two high pairs including aces is good since four of a kind and nut full house prospects exist, along with the chance of making a high straight. Flushes are also regular winners, so holding the A plus one other card of a particular suit again guarantees the nut flush if three or more cards of that suit are among the board cards. This is a better position to be in than when dealt four spades, as the reduced number of spades left in the deck makes a flush in that suit less likely. Similarly, when holding four cards in a sequence such as K, Q, J, 10, the hand is always stronger if two cards each from two suits are present to add flush and straight flush potential to that of making a straight.

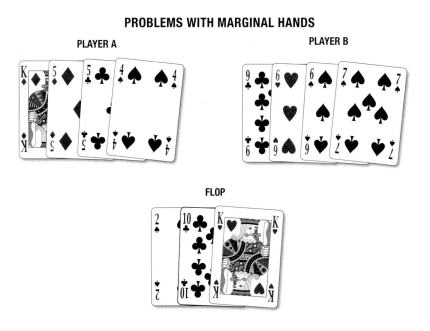

PROBLEMS WITH MARGINAL HANDS

PLAYER A

PLAYER B

FLOP

Above: Players with marginal hands need to be cautious when the board cards offer potential. Player A cannot use the K and the pair of fives simultaneously and has only a pair of kings, a weak hand on the flop. To make a winning hand requires two kings or two fives in the last two cards; should a K and 5 or K and 4 appear, the full house could lose to a player holding K, 10.

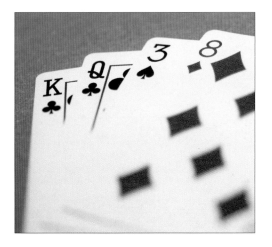

Left: The hole cards shown here represent a poor hand since only the Kc, Qc combination holds any real promise. Nevertheless, if the game features light betting and no pre-flop raises, as is customary when poker is played socially, hands such as these are much more likely to be retained than folded. A pair of eights on the flop, in this case, could then change the complexion of the hand altogether.

MORE COMBINATIONS

♦ ♣ ♥ ♠

Omaha games can feature up to ten players, this being the normal number for a cash game staged by a casino or online poker site. This many participants ensures that 40 cards – almost 80 per cent of the deck – are in play immediately after the deal and with each player forming six two-card combinations from their hole cards, 60 of these exist before the betting begins. This contributes to the typically high value of winning hands and underlines why players should always be trying to attain the best hand possible. However, while hands featuring high pairs, suited cards or connecting cards are favourable, even two-card combinations with modest potential regularly confound expectations. This is particularly true in fixed-limit Omaha games, when players with one decent two-card hand will often call to see the flop and find that their least valuable cards – 'rags' – suddenly become significant. For example a player holding Kc, Qc, 8d, 3s, would realistically expect only the K, Q combination to offer any chance of winning, but if the flop is 8h, 3d, Ks, then nine cards from the unseen 45 in the deck provide the player with a 38 per cent chance of achieving a full house. Any K, 8 or 3 will suffice, along with any two of the remaining three queens, although not all of these necessarily constitute the nuts. Should the turn and river cards be Kd and Ad, a player with a pair of aces or A, K would win, but the example does highlight the impact of having many more two-card combinations in play.

Post-flop strategy

Whatever the potential of a player's hole cards, the flop is the moment in the game when a hand's strength is clarified. Ideally, players will already have a mental picture of the cards they would prefer to see, although the principal consideration at this stage is the same as in Texas Hold 'em. In order to continue in the hand, players need to be confident that they have either the best hand or a realistic chance of achieving it.

This means identifying, first, which hand is likely to constitute the nuts and, second, whether it is possible to obtain it, given the cards at a player's disposal. Careless or inexperienced players are frequently seduced by the merits of a good hand only to discover, to their cost, that it is ultimately not good enough. As ever, a quick assessment of how many cards might make or break a hand, and the odds against them appearing, is crucial in determining whether to bet.

A player already holding the nuts can obviously focus on pot management and do whatever is required to keep opponents interested. They will often have sufficient scope for improvement to feel justified in calling a minimum bet to see the turn card. Loose players may even be prepared to call a raise in a fixed-limit game if they are slow to recognize that the nuts may already have been acquired. On the other hand, a check by the player holding a lock hand, which is essentially a hand that cannot lose, is likely to keep more opponents involved until later in the game, when the betting levels rise.

The aim then is to bet at the higher level and hope that opponents' hands have improved enough to call to see the final card. Should they do so, there is every chance they may call again in the fourth betting round, thus enhancing the profit made by slow-playing the nuts.

Above: Comic actor W.C. Fields keeps his cards close to his chest during a game. During his days in vaudeville in the early 20th century, Fields learned to play poker with some of the hustlers he met while touring, although golf was his preferred gambling medium. He did, however, develop some card tricks to supplement the skills he employed in his juggling act of the time.

COUNTING OUTS

FLOP

PLAYER A

PLAYER B

Above: These contrasting hands show the differing fortunes encountered as players consider the cards that can convert a hand into a winner. Player A has six chances of making a full house on the turn and 8 or 9 chances – depending on whether the turn card is an 8 – of filling it on the river, offering combined odds of just over 2 to 1 against. Player B has the best hand, but must assume that any pair on the board would be terminal. Of the unseen cards, 36 from the 45 remaining are good, and if the turn card pairs one of player B's hole cards, then 33 from the 44 in the deck are favourable. So player B has a 60 per cent chance of surviving both rounds.

Reading the cards

Once the flop has been revealed, players must note the possibilities presented by the three community cards. Any pair that appears will make it extremely likely that a full house or better will ultimately take the pot. Up to a third of all Omaha hands are won by full houses and half of these are likely to have been secured on the flop. Players with trips should therefore be wary of drawing to a full house that will not prove to be the best possible.

A flop featuring three cards of the same suit – Qc, 7c, 2c, for example – will stifle any betting from those who cannot beat a flush. A player holding the nut flush – perhaps Ac, 8c – should bet the maximum, since any caller is bound to be drawing for a full house and must be forced to pay for any of the cards that might complete it. When two cards to a flush appear on the flop, a player with the nut flush draw should also bet and hope for a couple of callers. When the flush is completed, the profits made will compensate for losses that occur when an opponent does hit a full house.

ESTIMATING PROBABILITIES ON THE FLOP
♦ ♣ ♥ ♠

Players are usually able to clarify their position after the flop to the extent that they can quickly calculate how many cards are either beneficial or detrimental to their prospects of winning the pot. Those needing two more cards to complete their hand will normally fold at this point, but players who recognize that any one of several cards will secure victory are more likely to continue. The key to any decision lies in the number of cards available that will confirm a player's hand as the winner. If any one of 13 cards from the unseen 45 will guarantee success, then a player has an even-money chance of taking the pot. Should there be more than 13 cards that will help, then the player is a slight favourite, while having less than 13 cards from which to draw a winner guarantees the player underdog status.

WHO IS FAVOURITE?

THE FLOP

PLAYER'S HAND

Above: After the flop, the key number for players to bear in mind is 13, since possessing this many outs for the best possible hand offers an even-money chance of victory. In this example, the player with the A-high straight can be certain of winning if any one of 15 cards appears on the turn or river, making the player a slight favourite to prevail.

Right: The player pictured here in possession of an A-high flush after the flop is in the perfect position to bet. Though holding the best hand, should either the turn or the river bring a card to pair one of those on the flop, it may be beaten by an opponent with a full house. A bet now would make it clear that the nut flush has been obtained which, if not sufficient to take the pot straight away, at least defines any callers as being in pursuit of a full house.

The turn

Since the flop offers so much information to the wary player, anyone still competing for the pot when the turn card is revealed must believe they have a potential winning hand, even if it has only an outside chance of success. After the turn card is dealt, the likely nature of the nuts should be apparent to all those still engaged in the game. This helps keep the basic analysis required to a minimum, since a player would only have three serious questions to consider before deciding whether a bet is warranted at this stage: do I have the best possible hand at the table, is it possible to obtain it, and does someone else already have it?

A player who is already in possession of the nuts should simply try to build the pot, while a player who identifies that the nut hand is still obtainable is justified in calling any opponent's bet when the pot odds are favourable. Meanwhile, those who recognize that their chances of catching a winning card on the river are poor in relation to the pot odds would probably do best to fold.

Above all, players must beware of calling a bet on the turn for a card that will improve their hand but not guarantee the win. Calling in the hope of making a K-high flush, for example, is usually the quickest way to discover an opponent has an A-high flush.

Estimating probabilities on the turn

Allowing the rules of probability to influence one's betting decisions is not always straightforward, even if it is generally advisable. With just one final community card to come, however, calculating the odds against seeing specific cards on the river, when the final community card is dealt, is relatively simple. Players who have leading hands will be considering how many cards might blend with the board to provide an opponent with a winning hand, while those drawing for cards will be making similar calculations regarding their own chances. Each hand represents a different puzzle, so players must be aware of the fluctuating probabilities apparent from one hand to the next. For example a player holding Ah, Kd, 10h, 10s when the board reads 3h, 8h, 4c, 5s has nine hearts remaining to make the nut flush, at odds of 4 to 1 against.

However, this would not be the best possible hand available if either the 4h or 5h completed the flush, because, by pairing the board, they could provide an opponent with a full house. To obtain the nuts and be certain of victory, the player must rely on the other seven hearts, at odds of just over 5 to 1 against. Should the board read 3h, 6h, 4c, 5s instead, then the chances of holding the nut hand if a heart appears on the river are reduced further. Although nine hearts still remain, the 2, 4, 5, and 7 all threaten

PLAYER C

HOLE CARDS

Right: To help visualize some of the strategic thinking that applies to Omaha, this example of a 100/200 fixed-limit game will highlight the betting decisions of player C in the big blind. The starting hand is good, with a high pair, a couple of connecting cards and two spades, offering multiple possibilities.

THE DEAL

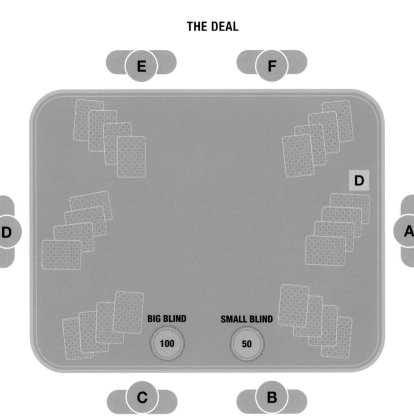

danger, since they have the potential to complete a low straight flush, while the full house options still exist. With only five cards that will guarantee the best hand, the player faces odds of 8 to 1 against this occurring.

AIMING STRAIGHT

♦ ♣ ♥ ♠

A straight is the minimum hand normally required to win the pot, although it can be difficult to exploit, given the frequency with which flushes and full houses occur in Omaha. Prior to the flop, the best chance of obtaining the hand arises when a player has a sequence of four consecutive hole cards, since this can complete up to 20 different straights, given the right board cards. A hand such as 9, 8, 7, 6, for instance, can make a Q-high straight with a Q, J, 10, or a 7-high straight with 5, 4, 3, and can work with 18 other three-card combinations to produce straights valued between these examples. On the flop, should there be no pair and no two cards of the same suit, there is an even-money possibility that a straight will ultimately win. However, players should still guard against finishing with anything less than the best possible straight available.

Left: A sequence of middle-ranking cards such as this is certainly worth playing if the pre-flop betting is light. There are 20 possible three-card combinations that could appear on the board to make a straight while the two hearts also offer flush possibilities. Despite the potential for making a strong hand, the low rank of the cards can cause problems. If the flop brought Q, J, 10, for example, the 9, 8 in the hole completes a straight, but this will be outranked by anyone holding K, 9 or A, K.

FIRST-ROUND BETTING

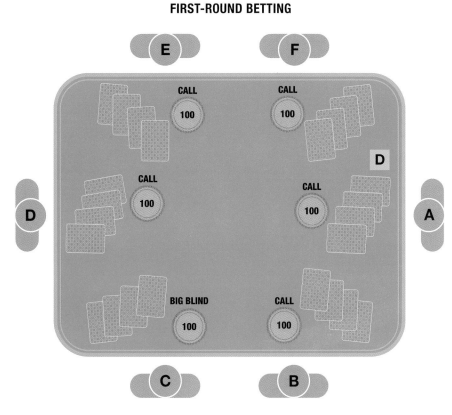

Left: Omaha characteristically features several players calling to see the flop, since even the weakest hand could quickly develop into an almost certain winner. For this reason, pre-flop raising in fixed-limit games is rare since it is unlikely to reduce the field sufficiently to make it worth the extra bet. Here, the remaining players all call the big blind (player C), who decides not to raise the betting further.

Call, bet or raise?

The flop may be the most crucial phase of the game, but the moment the turn card is revealed also prefaces a serious decision for those still contesting the pot. Players who can clearly see they have little chance of winning will probably fold, certainly in a fixed-limit game when it is normally impossible to bet enough to successfully bluff drawing hands out of contention.

Those whose hands still retain realistic prospects of taking the pot, by contrast, face a test of nerve and discipline as the serious betting begins. Not only is the minimum bet doubled on the turn in a typical Omaha game, but the likelihood is that players who bet now are probably committing themselves to further betting on the river. More bets generate bigger pots and this can tempt players into pursuing too many lost causes. Repeatedly finishing as the runner-up in these situations can reduce confidence as well as chip stacks.

In deciding whether to call, bet or even raise after the turn card has been dealt, good players will consider the pot odds on offer in light of the betting patterns throughout the game. Although betting without the best hand is usually ill advised, it is not always certain that an opponent already has it, with the clues behind this assessment coming from bets in the previous rounds. Despite the methodical approach recommended for playing Omaha successfully, being able to read an opponent's hand from the nature of the betting is a clear asset.

Right: As first person to act, player B surely indicates either a straight draw, two pairs or possession of a pocket pair – sevens or nines – that would make three of a kind. If this is so, then player C's winning full house possibilities are reduced, since the 7 or a 9 that could complete it might now give player B four of a kind. If player B has a Q, 9 or 9, 7, then the odds of 3 to 1 for securing a full house, although not the nuts, may well prompt a bet, too, given the pot odds. Player C's raise is a strong move and will have opponents pondering what the bet implies. Players F and B call the raise.

THE FLOP

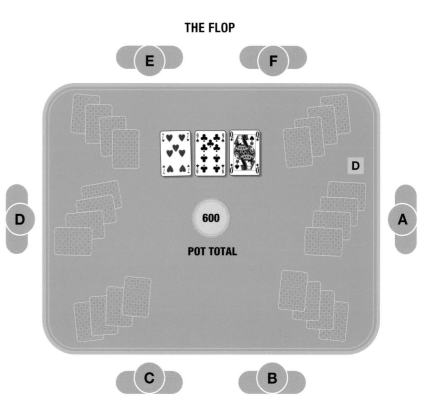

PLAYER C
HOLE CARDS

Above: The flop of 7, 9, Q is ideal for player C, who has the best hand with trip queens, and is just under 2 to 1 to make a full house or 'quads' (four of a kind) come the river card. Since the pot odds offer 6 to 1, maintaining interest in the hand is justified and a raise might eliminate a couple of opponents who missed the flop. Any 5, 6, 8, 10, J or K – 23 of the remaining 44 cards (player C has a K) – can fill a straight on the turn, however, and an opponent who does so will probably bet to try warding off draws for flushes and full houses.

SECOND BETTING ROUND

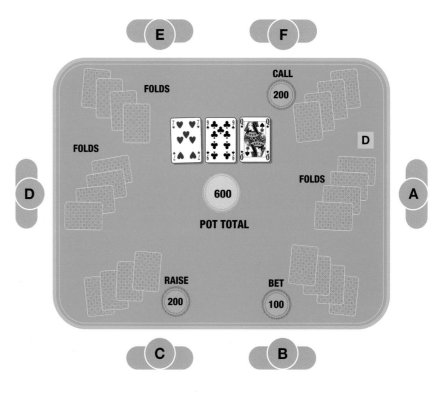

Passive or aggressive?

One of the things that makes Omaha such an enjoyable poker variation is that the many cards in circulation, particularly in a ten-player game, generate plenty of possibilities to make very strong hands. Betting tends to be lighter in the first two rounds, whether the game is fixed- or pot-limit poker, but becomes heavier from the turn onwards.

In pot-limit games, this is when the larger bets materialize, as players try to ward off those who, although possibly behind, still have chances to win. Such bets at this stage shrink the pot odds considerably, making speculative calls less attractive to opponents.

Yet large pots can still develop in fixed-limit poker, even though successful players are usually cautious and pragmatic. A couple of aggressive players who, on occasion, like to buck the odds with an irresponsible raise, can trigger an avalanche of betting in fixed-limit games. Since there are normally three or four raises per round before the betting level is capped, large pots can soon develop if a betting war breaks out. Under such circumstances, the implied pot odds on offer might tempt even the most passive player into calling for the river card if any chance of winning exists.

Simple decisions

Players whose betting on the turn is governed by the probabilities at work can expect to save themselves plenty of chips if they are strictly disciplined in their approach. The key is counting exactly how many of the unseen cards can help them either retain or acquire the winning hand. With four cards on the board and four in the hand, each player knows the value of eight cards. Simply, if half the remaining 44 cards will provide a player with a winning hand, then the chances are evidently even that this will happen, making any bet or call almost obligatory.

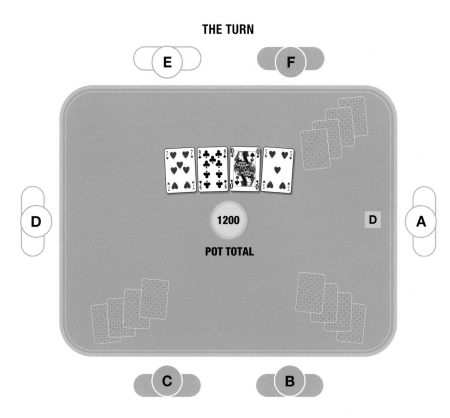

THE TURN

1200

POT TOTAL

Above: The 5h on the turn does not improve player C's hand but can do little either for any opponent holding a pair of nines or sevens in the hole. It does help fulfil a low straight for any opponent holding 8, 6, which is plausible given that these two cards could feature in the hand of someone also holding a high pair such as aces or kings, for example.

If only 11 cards will confirm the hand as a winner, then the odds against it occurring are 3 to 1, which might discourage a player from calling a bet in a very tight game. Players with fewer than 11 cards working for them should definitely be sure that the pot odds on offer will justify staying for the river, in the face of any bet.

Above: The pair of sevens supplemented by the A, 10 suited represents a fair starting hand and it is just one combination that could plausibly be held by player B in the game illustrated on these pages. From player C's perspective, player B's bet into a flop showing 7, 9, Q could easily be construed as representing trip sevens though this is a hand player C has well covered at present with the trip queens.

The river

The card that completes the deal and removes all doubt regarding the value of a player's hand and how it compares with the best available, is the river card. At this point it is worth reiterating the golden rule of Omaha, which underlines how the game essentially amounts to a search for the nuts. Any player who does not hold the best possible hand available after the river card may safely assume that an opponent probably does.

If the betting patterns suggest exactly that, then there is little sense in a player calling a last-round bet, however modest, in order to confirm what is already suspected. This applies to both fixed- and pot-limit games, although players are more likely to support potentially strong hands on the flop or the turn in pot-limit Omaha with large bets, offering clues to the value of their cards. Having been called as far as the river, a modest final-round bet by a player who had raised in the previous round should create suspicion in the mind of an opponent who has failed to make a lock hand. The possibility exists that the opponent is being trapped into parting with a few more chips by a player with the nuts.

THIRD BETTING ROUND

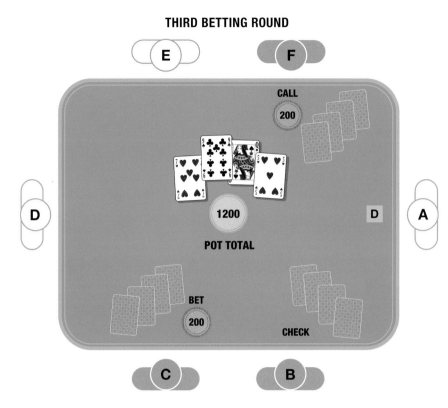

Above: The raise from Player C after the flop causes player B to check this time round after the turn card is dealt, either to re-examine the possibilities presented by the board or, perhaps, to set a trap. Player C bets the minimum, reasoning that player B could be slow-playing a straight by holding an 8 and 6, but that it is still more likely he has three of a kind. If this is the case, then another 7 or 9 on the river could be disastrous for player C since either card could conceivably furnish player B with four of a kind. In the event, players F and B both call, but do not raise, indicating possession of hands that probably still require improvement.

PLAYER C
HOLE CARDS

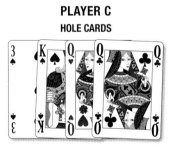

Right: Three players are still competing as the river card falls, giving player C the nuts with four of a kind. Although opponents may have read the betting patterns correctly and put player C on pocket queens, the pair on the board could have made someone a full house that may induce them to bet. Although four of a kind is not uncommon in Omaha, players find it difficult to fold a hand as good as a full house. Once player B checks, player C has no option but to bet and hope for a call to swell the pot. With the best hand, there is no point checking and allowing opponents a free showdown.

THE RIVER

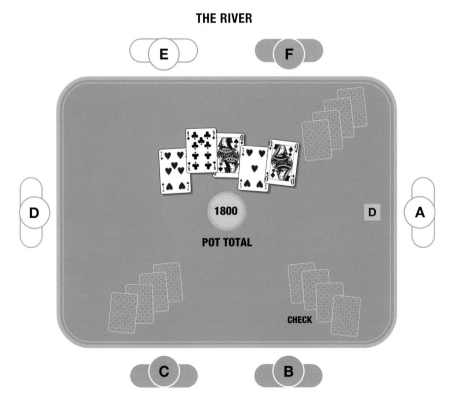

Reading opponents

Identifing the contrasting levels of players' skills is an essential element of successful poker, as is assessing their motivations. While Omaha strategy involves some inflexible rules, players are still challenged psychologically to decipher the meaning behind any bet after the river card has been dealt.

Having survived three rounds of betting, players hope their efforts have been worthwhile, even when evidence from the cards alone suggests this is unlikely. But the winning hand is not always the best possible, especially when several low cards are featured in the widow. Potential lock hands may have been folded, leaving perhaps the most aggressive players to fight over the spoils with reasonable but not outstanding cards. A player facing an awkward decision on the river should reconsider the scale and timing of previous bets. Players who raised on the flop, for example, may have done so in order to eliminate several dangers to a weak leading hand. If the hand implied by that bet does not appear to have been strengthened by the turn and river cards, the bet could have been a semi-bluff that failed to pay off.

Large bets from players after the turn card ordinarily imply that they hold the nut hand or are strong favourites to do so on the river. But since the inference is easily understood by experienced Omaha players, some may choose to capitalize on this awareness by occasionally prosecuting a bluff.

Pot management

Players lucky enough to have a winning opportunity early in the hand are in prime position to control the betting. They can exercise more choice in whether to raise a pot and eliminate potential threats or conceal the value of their cards by calling along with several opponents. The time for setting a trap may arise later, when an opponent stumbles across a good hand that is destined to lose. For example a player holding Ac, Ah, Jd, 8d will appreciate the promise presented by a flop of 10d, As, 9d. In early position, a check may be in order to see how many opponents also like the flop, with anyone holding trips, two pairs and draws for high flushes likely to bet or call the minimum.

If a call will then suffice to see the turn card, the hand may be underrated by opponents who might have expected a player holding trip aces to have advertised the fact already. Should the turn card be the Ad, prompting a bet from the player now holding four aces, anyone with a full house – by matching a pair of tens, perhaps – may call a bet for fear of being bluffed out of a win. All the time they are drawing dead while the player with the top hand is patiently encouraging them to build the pot. In this position, the player would like to see a 10 or a 9 on the river, since that could give an opponent a lower-ranking four of a kind that would prove very difficult to fold, despite the implications behind the player's betting becoming more clear.

FINAL BETTING ROUND

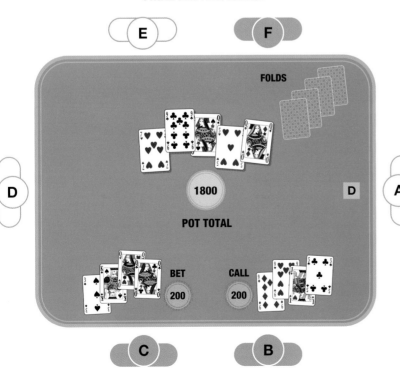

Left: Player C's bet is enough to persuade player F to fold, but player B calls the 200 only to discover that the full house of nines over queens is outranked. This is a common mistake among Omaha players, who are often sufficiently seduced by the size of the pot that they will commit more chips despite knowing they could be beaten. In pot-limit games, players may be more inclined to bluff without the nuts, but, even when suspecting a bluff, calling a large bet with a beatable hand is a tough decision.

ONLINE POKER

The huge surge of interest in poker during the past decade is attributable almost entirely to the increased publicity for the game generated by television and the Internet. As the intricacies of tournament-style Texas Hold 'em entertained and inspired television viewers, so online poker sites emerged to offer convenient and ready access to a game. PlanetPoker started the trend in 1998 and there are now over 600 online gaming companies offering access to the top 40 poker networks, generating revenue of over US$100 billion per year. Such sums have attracted many of the world's leading companies from the betting industry and beyond, all establishing their own online poker rooms in their eagerness for a piece of the increasingly lucrative action. However, this rapid growth has understandably brought with it a degree of concern over the morality of gambling online, as well as prompting investigations into its legality. These issues and some basic details regarding the online poker experience are the subject of this chapter.

Right: The upsurge in interest in the game of poker can be squarely placed on the shoulders of rapid developments in the media. As soon as poker tournaments started being televised, the game's legendary players became more widely known and the subsequent inundation of poker guidebooks helped generate even more publicity for the game. The Internet not only offers access to virtually everything there is to know about poker, but also acts as a barometer of poker's global popularity.

THE LAW AND ONLINE POKER

The speed at which online poker has developed as a hugely popular global gambling medium has, to some extent, left the machinations of the law far behind in many countries, and the extensive reach of the Internet has thrown these differences into stark relief.

For the most part, governments of nations in Europe, South America, Asia and around the Caribbean have either adopted a pragmatic approach by legalizing online gambling, or have actively welcomed gaming companies by licensing their operations. However, in America, home to over half of online poker players, the confusion surrounding the legality of Internet betting came to a head in October 2006. Repeated attempts by right-wing Republicans to lobby for an outright ban proved successful when President George W. Bush signed the Safe Port Act, enacting a law that ostensibly aimed to improve American port security. A late amendment to the bill meant that the Unlawful Internet Gambling Enforcement Act was simultaneously incorporated into the legislation. The principal thrust of this additional act is to restrict financial institutions from processing transactions to and from the now outlawed Internet gaming sites on behalf of their clients. Consequently, although online poker itself is not specifically illegal, players based in America are effectively prevented from utilizing their online betting accounts which obviously reduces the incentive to play. Needless to say, both the online gaming companies and the vast army of online poker players are working towards overturning this legislation, their primary argument being that poker is a game of skill and not pure chance.

Above: The security and integrity of online casino operations is becoming increasingly trustworthy thanks to the fierce competition between companies offering the service. It is in their interests to make the financial dealings as simple and secure as possible. This includes offering players the option to restrict their involvement in games by means of responsible game settings.

Right: Don't get in trouble with the law! Collusion can be a problem in both real world and virtual poker rooms, and involves two or more players working together to gain an unfair advantage. However, online casino companies operate sophisticated security software that is designed to police collusive behaviour or fraudulent activity by monitoring playing patterns.

Regulations

Unsurprisingly, considering America's current responses to online gaming, very few countries are prepared to provide licences to online casinos and poker rooms, with most operations being concentrated in places such as Costa Rica, Gibraltar, Malta and countries dotted around the Caribbean. The UK, with one eye on the potential tax revenues that might accrue, has legalized the establishment of online gaming sites, and this move is considered likely to instil more confidence in the industry among consumers.

Although it is true that reputable companies pay their host country a sizeable licensing fee and subject their operations to official scrutiny, the fact remains that the industry itself is mostly self-regulating. Several organizations monitor online gaming, of which the Interactive Gaming Council, Online Players' Association and Gambling Commission are perhaps most respected. In a competitive market, the vast majority of operators recognize that customer satisfaction is of paramount importance and promote the integrity of their businesses. Some rogue elements do still exist, and it is incumbent on the consumer to exercise a degree of caution when selecting an Internet site at which to play.

Online security

Although one cannot be assured of the security of online poker sites in view of the rapidly changing world of computer technology, the majority can be trusted to handle financial transactions and keep personal details confidential. The digital encryption methods are the same as those used by the world's financial institutions and it is in the interests of the operators to ensure that security is watertight.

The better sites monitor the virtual tables for signs of players cheating by colluding with each other during a game. Two or three players could gain a seat at the same table and communicate with each other about their respective hands remotely. High-stakes games are more likely to be targeted by cheats, but the better poker sites operate systems that identify suspect betting patterns. Players who suspect cheating can always alert the operator's customer support section. It may not compensate any immediate losses, but it will prompt the most reputable online poker rooms to investigate.

GETTING STARTED

The online poker market is immensely competitive, with literally hundreds of sites offering the chance for players to indulge their passion. Three years after the launch of PlanetPoker, PartyPoker became the dominant force in the industry on the back of a major advertising campaign in 2003 that helped it command almost half the total revenues generated by the online game. Following the implementation of the Unlawful Internet Gambling Enforcement Act in October 2006, however, PartyPoker's decision to withdraw its services to American customers led to PokerStars assuming the mantle of busiest poker site. Here, the big-money tournaments are renowned as being among the toughest to win. It is also the site from which which both Chris Moneymaker and Greg Raymer emerged to become WSOP world champions and, not surprisingly, it has a reputation for attracting solid and experienced players.

Other online poker rooms worthy of mention are Full Tilt Poker, Titan Poker and Pacific Poker, since these are also well regarded within the industry. Many of the sites are endorsed by poker professionals, while Doyle Brunson is just one player to exploit his reputation for integrity by creating his own online poker room.

Registration

Logging on to a preferred site is a straightforward process for anyone familiar with accessing the Internet. In order to play, however, it is necessary to register with the operator, which will involve submitting an email address, selecting a username and creating a password. An account number will be issued, although it is not always necessary to make an immediate cash deposit in order to be able to play, since there are usually play money tables in operation. Details of the account and access to the virtual poker tables can only be obtained by submitting the relevant username and password. It is not unusual for players to have accounts with several online poker rooms, so it is advisable to keep a separate record of the account numbers and passwords for each. The majority of sites require players to download the necessary software before being able to play, but several still offer the chance to play within a web browser.

Below: Four of the more established online gaming sites available today. There are over 140 sites catering for players seeking a game in the comfort of their own home. The astonishing growth in online poker is a 21st-century phenomenon, the first online card room opening just before the millennium.

Below: Poker is growing fast in Germany, with nearly 300,000 players logging on to gaming sites, despite a change to German law in January 2008 effectively banning online betting. Deutsche Poker Tour is a free online poker league whose members play on poker sites to gain points that will enable them to compete for the huge prize pool on offer at the league championship.

Above: Armed with a low-grade personal computer (PC), a 56K modem and access to a telephone line, it is possible to play poker games with people all over the world. The benefit that online poker offers the novice is the chance to practise, without the trouble of finding a card room or organizing a game.

Navigating the virtual poker room

Rival sites differ cosmetically in terms of their graphics and presentation but access to the desired games and ancillary services is generally organized along very similar lines. Drop-down menus and clearly labelled tabs indicate the poker variations available, the stake levels that apply and the betting structures that are in operation. Distinguishing between cash games and tournaments is simple and there are a range of statistical details available for each table in operation including such key information as the average pot size and the number of hands dealt per hour. This can help a player to identify whether a game is tight or loose which is useful in formulating an initial strategy.

Once seated at a table, of course, a player must actively click on the relevant button to join a game at which point such elements as the deal and the payment of antes is automated. The options available to each player when a betting decision needs to be made are clearly displayed and only require the press of a button or a click of the mouse to check, bet or fold.

POKERBOTS
♦ ♣ ♥ ♠

All serious poker players are keen on having an edge over their opponents, and online players are no different. To this end, many are inclined to employ pokerbots, these being computer software programs that can access a game in progress and provide a player with a range of useful information. Pokerbots can read all the face-up cards and calculate pot odds as well as make recommendations on which hands to play and when to bet. In this regard, they can save a player time in making a decision, although it might be argued that this stunts the development of an individual's own ability to read a game. Some pokerbots can be programmed to play automatically, but their success rates are rather limited.

Modest returns at low-stakes games have been recorded, but, given the rigid strategies often employed by the pokerbots, this success is often attributed to the poor quality of the players that contest such games. Experienced players are better able to manipulate a hand when playing a predictable opponent, and, as yet, no pokerbot program is able to understand the subtleties of bluffing and checkraising to pose a serious threat.

ONLINE GAMES

Despite some variations from one card room to another, the mainstays of online poker are Texas Hold 'em, Omaha and seven-card stud, along with the split-pot games Omaha/8 and seven-card stud high/low. Draw poker is also available at some sites as is the Hold 'em derivative, crazy pineapple, a game in which players are dealt three cards rather than two, one of which must be discarded following the flop and the conclusion of the second betting round. Such is the scale of American influence on the game that the majority of sites trade in US dollars, irrespective of their registered location.

The betting structures operated are the staples of fixed-limit, pot-limit and no-limit, with the former recommended as the most likely to appeal to the beginner. Games for real money exist at levels ranging from a few cents up to hundreds of dollars and should easily match the means of anybody who wishes to play. Of course, the key difference when playing poker in a virtual card room compared to the live experience is that the pace of events is much quicker. Each hand may take less than a minute to complete and players rarely have the luxury of sitting back for more than 30 seconds to contemplate a decision.

Left: A leading Japanese online poker guide, featuring reviews of all major poker rooms, top lists, strategy advice for both beginners and advanced players as well as poker rules. It also offers daily freerolls and tournament schedules. The nation of 128 million is looking to lift its ban on casinos to increase tourist arrivals and revive its gaming industry. Japan's ruling party is holding talks with global gaming companies including Harrah's Entertainment Inc. to operate the nation's first casinos after 2010.

Right: Juega Poker Ya is one of Spain's leading online poker gaming sites offering freeroll and satellite tournaments. Thousands of budding Spanish poker players are queuing up to learn how to play in the hope of emulating the success of Spanish poker star Carlos Mortensen, World Poker Champion in 2001. Poker is similar to the popular Spanish gambling game Mus, another game of skill and psychology where players try to outwit their opponents.

Left: There are many online poker gaming sites in Russia, though Malta-based company Red Star Poker, which opened in June 2005, filled the crucial void of providing instruction and customer service in both Russian and English. Upon downloading the necessary gaming software, players may participate in satellite tournaments with international players.

Slovenska poker stran

Above: An online poker gaming site in Slovenia. Casinos in Slovenia are attracting gamblers from Italy, where tight marketing restrictions and high tax rates have hampered growth in the industry. In 2004, over 87 per cent of all visits to Slovenian casinos were made by foreigners.

Above: An Israeli poker portal, in Hebrew. Gambling is currently illegal in Israel, but there are efforts to reverse that. The Israeli government is sitting on a proposal that would allow casinos to be built in Eilat, the country's principal holiday city. A formal decision has yet to be made, but many groups of investors are already vying for building contracts.

How many players?

In keeping with the standard tables in the card rooms and casinos of the world, online poker tables typically have space for nine or ten players. Texas Hold 'em and Omaha are the games most likely to accommodate the maximum per table, while seven-card stud games are usually limited to eight players. All these games, are also staged with lower limits on the number of participants, with heads-up contests widely available and many Texas Hold 'em tables limited to three, four or five players. The impact of having fewer competitors is that the blinds circulate the table quicker, of course, and this keeps players involved in the action. With the standard of the average winning hand also being reduced, such short-handed games tend to be loose betting affairs and appeal to those who perhaps do not have the patience or inclination to fold a succession of hands while watching others compete.

The rake

This is the fee charged by the online poker room for providing the facilities to play. To enter a US$10 tournament, for example, players are usually required to pay US$11, of which US$10 goes into the prize pool with the additional US$1 being claimed by the operator. A levy of ten per cent is typical for the lower-stakes games although it is often reduced in more expensive tournaments.

The fees that are charged in cash games differ quite considerably from site to site with levels varying from five to ten per cent of each pot at the lowest stake levels. A cap is often placed on the rake if a pot exceeds

PLAY-MONEY POKER
♦ ♣ ♥ ♠

Once registered to an online poker site, players will normally be credited with chips that may be used in play-money games only. These offer an ideal opportunity for novices to learn how to play at no expense and so represent a valuable educational resource. Experienced players may also find them useful as a means of warming up prior to sitting in on a real money game. Obviously, with nothing at stake, the games tend to be fairly loose affairs, but that does not diminish their potential for helping a player focus on the key facets of the game prior to playing for real.

a certain size but the poker room's cut could easily be a dollar or more for every hand. Since 60 hands per hour is a fairly common rate of play per table, the scale of the potential income to be accrued becomes apparent given the thousands of virtual tables simultaneously staging a game at any one time.

From a consumer's perspective it is obviously worth checking the rake charts that are published by the majority of reputable online poker rooms. A comparison between the different rates applicable at the preferred betting levels will certainly prove worthwhile for anyone considering playing for several hours a week. Even those who win consistently may be paying more for the privilege than need be the case.

CASH GAMES

One of the great advantages of online poker is the sheer wealth of information available to players who wish to engage in a cash game. Those with some experience of the medium will consider the statistics for each table at the betting level they favour, taking into account such information as the average pot size and, at Texas Hold 'em tables, how many players are seeing the flop, usually expressed in percentage terms. A loose table can be identified as one where at least half the players are regularly calling to see the flop, probably with some modest hands among them. Such a game would be a very attractive proposition for an experienced poker player who is able to exercise more discipline in selecting which hands to support. Games with a minimum bet of US$1 or more can normally be expected to attract reasonably good players, whereas the levels below this appeal more to those who treat their poker casually.

Understanding the likely quality of opposition is a key consideration, of course, with many online players content to compete without a solid appreciation of strategy and the nuances of a particular game. Identifying these players can certainly help, but unsophisticated opponents pose problems in that they are difficult to bluff, being unable to understand the

implications behind a strong bet. Similarly, any calling stations or maniacs at the table who are content to play many hands cannot beat the odds in the long run but will, on occasions, strike it lucky by hitting the cards they need to win. Such players are hazardous, but not as daunting as those who sit patiently, folding hand after hand while waiting for the cards that will justify a large bet. Becoming involved in betting confrontations with tight, aggressive players should only be considered when holding an exceptionally good hand.

Stake levels

A minimum and maximum buy-in normally applies at whichever table one chooses to play, particularly in pot-limit and no-limit games, while in fixed-limit, poker players may be able to buy in for their entire bankroll. Ordinarily, the upper limit is one hundred times the minimum bet and it is recommended that players always buy in for the maximum permitted. Maintaining a chip stack that is well in excess of the average pot size at the table is essential to ward off pressure from the chip leaders and to ensure that, in the event of holding a winning hand, a player can capitalize on it to best advantage. Topping up one's chip stack where permitted is therefore advisable,

Left: There has been a huge upsurge in people playing poker online globally and the Eastern European nation, Croatia, is no exception. On land, the country boasts 12 casinos, of which four are located in Zagreb, the capital city. The largest casino in the country, Miro hotel and casino Minera in Plovanija, has 34 gaming tables and 250 video poker or other gaming machines.

Right: An online poker gaming website in Chinese. ESPN, an American cable TV network dedicated to sports-related programming is the major broadcaster of poker. The sports network now airs in China and has exposed 1.3 billion people to the game. The first to feel these benefits will be the online gaming sites.

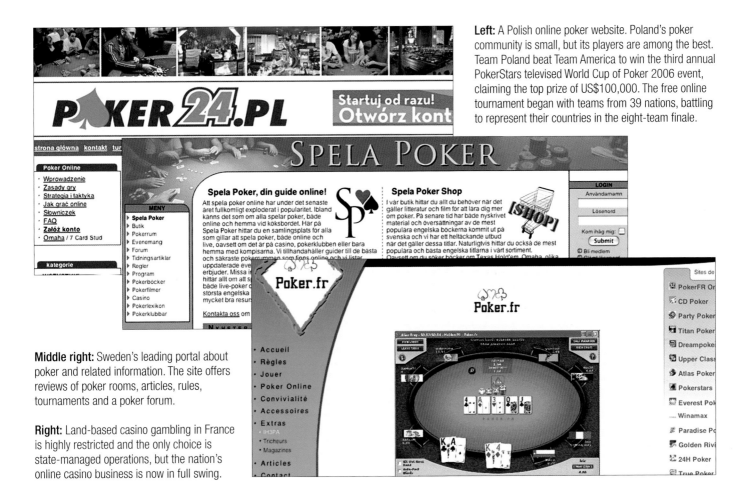

Left: A Polish online poker website. Poland's poker community is small, but its players are among the best. Team Poland beat Team America to win the third annual PokerStars televised World Cup of Poker 2006 event, claiming the top prize of US$100,000. The free online tournament began with teams from 39 nations, battling to represent their countries in the eight-team finale.

Middle right: Sweden's leading portal about poker and related information. The site offers reviews of poker rooms, articles, rules, tournaments and a poker forum.

Right: Land-based casino gambling in France is highly restricted and the only choice is state-managed operations, but the nation's online casino business is now in full swing.

although there is little point in continually doing so at a table where an opponent has amassed a chip lead of perhaps two or three times the maximum buy-in.

Similarly, players should be incredibly confident in their ability to consider joining a table where one opponent already has such an advantage. It is usually indicative of having played well for several hours, and confronting an in-form opponent with the means to make intimidating bets is inadvisable in the extreme.

Online poker tells

The ability to read opponents in order to assess the meaning behind any bet is an asset and, to this end, deciphering clues from a player's body language can often be helpful. However, distinctive physical mannerisms are quite obviously not visible when playing online, although there are still some clues available to the keen observer regarding opponents' styles and attitudes.

Messages in the chat box, if taken at face value, might prove a good indicator of an opponent's mood, given that many players could easily be tired, bored or even drunk. During a game there are some who take the maximum permitted time to make a decision, which could be the result of a poor connection, but could also indicate that the individual concerned is either a novice or is playing several tables simultaneously. If the latter is suspected, the opponent may be restricting play to aggressive support for premium starting hands at each table as that is a much easier strategy to manage. Any bet or raise from such an opponent would evidently merit respect under these circumstances. Similarly, an opponent who raises a bet almost instantaneously usually indicates possession of a good hand, the speed of the response suggesting maximum confidence. Conversely, an opponent who takes much more time than usual in playing one particular hand may be consciously trying to disguise its true value.

Online poker rooms do offer the facility for players to make notes about their opponents while games are in progress, and many offer a statistical breakdown of one's own play during any session. However, the speed of the games themselves and the tendency for virtual tables to experience a high turnover of players makes it difficult to read opponents. Taking note of new players joining the table and adjusting one's strategy accordingly is crucial to success at the online game.

ONLINE TOURNAMENTS

The inspiration provided by the spectacle of televised tournament poker is undoubtedly responsible for the popularity of the knockout game in online poker rooms. While trying to make a regular profit from cash games requires a long-term strategy and a consistently disciplined approach, the appeal of tournament poker is that a single victory could realize a dramatic profit for a few hours' work. In addition, because the entry fees are always stipulated, it is possible to know in advance the maximum loss that will be incurred if a player is knocked out before reaching the prize-money positions.

One other aspect of tournaments that makes them so appealing to the new generation of poker players is that luck has the potential to undermine the strategies of opponents who are regarded as more skilful. One bad beat and the loss of a substantial pot can seriously undermine a good player's attempts to win a tournament as easily as those of a novice. However, it must be remembered that the very best professionals regularly finish in the prize money in live tournaments so there is no reason to suppose that experienced online tournament players are not similarly successful, particularly in the high-stakes contests.

Tournament structures

The very nature of online poker permits a greater range of tournament styles and structures than might be found in a typical card room, such are the benefits of having a computer program in control of proceedings. The single-table sit 'n' go tournaments for between five and ten players are especially popular, since they rarely take more than an hour to complete at most. Indeed, if played as high-speed turbo tournaments, they may be resolved in less than half that time.

At the other end of the scale, the multi-table tournaments hosted by online poker rooms can take several hours to complete, making them more appealing to players with time on their hands. Texas Hold 'em is the preferred game for most online tournament players, although other popular variations are also played in tournament format using the standard range of betting structures.

Strategic considerations

In terms of actual tournament strategy, the basic advice is for players to be cautiously disciplined during the early stages while taking stock of opponents, only betting when in possession of a very good hand.

Left: The computer age may soon be creeping into card rooms, and taking jobs from dealers. Here a game of Texas Hold 'em is being played on the new PokerPro dealer-free electronic poker tables at the Hollywood Park Casino in Inglewood, California. The electronic tables require no dealers, as the players select all their actions via the touch screen in front of them. The casino unveiled its e-poker room in October 2006, making it the first casino in California to feature e-poker tables which combine the speed and accuracy of online poker with the personal player interaction of traditional 'brick and mortar' casino poker.

Left and below: All Aussie Poker is an Australian online poker resource, offering a range of poker-related services; Mega poker is its Dutch equivalent. Type in 'online poker' to almost any search engine and and you will score a barrage of hits.

Below right: The convenience and anonymity associated with playing online poker has led to women representing roughly 40 per cent of the card-room clientele, compared to just 5 per cent in real life card rooms and casinos.

All players start with the same number of chips, but this selective approach can help to conserve a player's resources while opponents knock each other out.

From the middle stages onwards, players need to be selectively more aggressive in order to withstand the increasing betting levels, this being easier for those in healthy chip positions, of course. Varying one's playing style to accommodate the changing fortunes of opponents is a requirement at this point, and those with the largest stacks are obviously in a position to take a few more risks with moderate hands without necessarily damaging their overall prospects.

By the time the tournament reaches its final stages, betting choices are often dictated by the size of a player's chip stack as much as by the cards themselves. Those in the lead will be pressurizing those with fewer chips and on the verge of elimination in order to move one step nearer the top prize. Understandably, it is this level of volatility at the business end of the event that makes tournament poker so exciting for regular participants.

PRIZES
♦ ♣ ♥ ♠

Prize money is normally distributed among the leading ten per cent of players in any tournament, though some events are organized on a 'winner takes all' basis. A single-table tournament of ten players will usually see the first three rewarded, the winner taking 50 per cent of the prize pool. A US$10 event will see the winner claiming US$50, the runner-up US$30 and third-place US$20. Multi-table events featuring 1,000 entrants could see the winner's share reduced to 25 per cent of the total prize pool, to accommodate payments for the top 100 finishers. Assuming a US$10 event once more, the first prize would still amount to US$2,500, which is an attractive sum for a modest outlay. However, beating up to 1,000 opponents in a hugely competitive environment is obviously a major achievement and not something that many poker players are regularly able to repeat.

Casinos and Clubs

The recent popularity of playing online poker over the last decade has created an increased demand for the game in the world's foremost casinos, although many of the smaller establishments are still reluctant to provide poker facilities. From a purely commercial perspective, the cost of operating a poker table is rarely as profitable for the house as a range of other gambling games such as roulette, craps or the ubiquitous slot machines. In these, of course, players bet against the house rather than each other, assuring the casinos of a regular and predictable stream of income. However, despite the fact that the rake from a poker table may never match the revenue of a dozen slot machines that could easily take its place, consumer demand has helped prompt a change of approach. As a result, the opportunity to play the game in public has attracted many more poker players into the casinos of the world. For those new to the experience, this chapter highlights some of the key factors to bear in mind when playing poker in a commercial card room.

Right: In poker, the cards are shuffled prior to the deal of each hand. The players will normally shuffle and deal in home games and smaller clubs, while in casinos it is more likely that a dealer will be employed specifically to manage this aspect of the game. A professional dealer can help to speed up proceedings, leaving players free to concentrate on their poker strategies although this luxury comes at a price in the form of the casino rake, a fee often levied on each pot to cover the costs of the dealer and other facilities.

WHAT TO EXPECT

Players who are used to enjoying poker in home games against friends, particularly for modest stakes, are entitled to be intimidated when they first venture into a dedicated poker room. Of course, the setting will differ from one card room to another, with the glitz and glamour of the palatial hotel-casinos in Las Vegas not replicated in small, urban poker clubs. There may be five tables in operation or 50, but the fact remains that anyone who takes a seat in a commercial card room for the first time, to play poker against complete strangers, is likely to feel nervous.

The unfamiliar environment, the potential distractions and the need to keep stock of developments at the table can all conspire to disrupt a player's concentration. This, of course, can prove costly, so those considering a visit to a card room are well advised to familiarize themselves with the venue for a while before engaging in a game. There will always be members of staff on hand to answer any questions concerning the facilities on offer and the general rules that apply to specific games. Most poker commentators suggest that it is always a good idea to watch a game in progress for a while rather than take a seat immediately, should one be available. This helps acclimatize a player to the environment and offers the chance to gauge the quality of the opposition and the style of the games in progress.

Above: The Bellagio hotel and casino, Las Vegas, was inspired by the Lake Como resort of Bellagio in Italy. It was the most expensive hotel ever built when opened in 1998, having cost over US$1.6 billion. Many professional poker players prefer to play there, due in part to the high table limits.

House rules

Every poker room will have a manager, cashiers and a set of rules governing the games, as well as points of general etiquette. Larger operations will, of course, employ several dealers and have staff on hand to deal with any disputes as they arise. Although a degree of consistency is common in card rooms operating in close proximity to each other, there are often variations governing the betting limits, the permitted buy-ins and the structures of the games. Few people are likely to play poker in a formal setting without having some experience of the game, but it is still incumbent upon the individual to be aware of the different regulations in operation.

It is also worth remembering that experienced players prefer a fairly swift pace to proceedings and, because of the rake and the potential for earning tips, dealers are inclined to meet this demand. Inexperienced players can soon become a nuisance to opponents and dealers alike if they continually struggle to follow events and delay the game by seeking continual guidance on what options are available to them. This underlines how harshly competitive the game can be when played in a commercial setting and confirms the need for proper preparation on the part of any prospective participant.

Left: Laser light show at the Las Vegas Golden Nugget casino-hotel. The world's largest gold nugget on display, the Hand of Faith, is in the lobby. Weighing 876 troy ounces (27.2kg) and 46 centimetres (18 inches) in length, it was found near the Golden Triangle in Australia in 1980.

Right: The famous 'Welcome to Las Vegas' sign, located just to the south of the Las Vegas Strip. Betty Willis and Ted Rogich created the sign, characteristic of the Googie architecture movement popular at the time, for Clark County, Nevada. The back of the sign reads 'Drive Carefully and Come Back Soon'. When seen up close, the circles on which the letters of the word 'WELCOME' appear reveal themselves to be silver dollars.

Las Vegas

Poker's long association with Las Vegas has helped it develop a magnetic appeal that attracts players from all over the world. The choice of games and venues on offer is staggering, with over 50 dedicated card rooms catering for their needs. Many, such as the Bellagio, the Mirage and Caesar's Palace, are located in the plush casinos of the Las Vegas Strip, while Binion's Horseshoe, the former home of the WSOP, is in the downtown area, along with the Golden Nugget. Although each poker room has its own unique personality, there are aspects common to all, with relaxed dress codes the norm and, increasingly, a ban on smoking at the poker tables. Not surprisingly, many of the world's best poker players live and work in Las Vegas and anyone seriously considering a visit can expect fierce competition in whichever room they choose to play.

BINION'S, LAS VEGAS
♦ ♣ ♥ ♠

For many, this is the only place to play poker, such is the casino's famous association with the WSOP, instigated by the venue's original owner, Benny Binion. Originally known as Binion's Horseshoe, the casino was rebranded following a change of ownership, while the WSOP has moved to Harrah's Rio Casino, having outgrown its original home. Situated at 128 East Fremont, Binion's has 14 tables in a room regarded as spacious by casino standards, with the usual roster of Texas Hold 'em, seven-card stud and Omaha. Betting limits are among the lowest in town, with US$2/$4 fixed-limit Texas Hold 'em on offer, while the minimum buy-in for a no-limit game is US$100, the blinds being set at US$1 and US$2. No-limit Texas Hold 'em tournaments are organized daily, the buy-ins starting at US$50 – plus US$10 for administration – although the cost rises to US$150 plus US$30 on Friday and Saturday evenings. Basic lessons in how to play Texas Hold 'em are held at 11am each day.

Right: Binion's Horsehoe casino, located in the centre of Fremont Street, where two million light bulbs and 540,000 watts of sound transform the canopy into the world's largest animated light show every night. Although it is most famous for its gaming, the Horseshoe has other popular attractions, including the Poker Hall of Fame wall inside, which honours the greatest players in the history of poker.

THE CASINO RAKE

As mentioned earlier, while poker clubs do exist, many established international casinos have at times been reluctant to offer players the facilities required to pursue their preferred gambling interest. The resurgence of interest in the game has encouraged a change of heart in many cases, but the services provided by any commercial card room do come at a price, of course. This takes the form of the 'rake', sometimes referred to as the 'cut', the 'vigorish' or 'vig'. It is usually set at a minimum of three per cent, and could be as high as ten per cent of every pot contested, although there will usually be a cap on the rake once any pot exceeds a certain level.

Given that it is often customary for the winner of each pot to tip the dealer, it soon becomes evident how difficult it is to make money from the game. This is particularly the case at the lower-stake levels, where, even when capped, the rake can seem a relatively big slice of the smaller pots usually contested. Winning an average number of pots may not be enough to break even unless players limit themselves to playing hands that promise an early advantage. Exerting this discipline requires folding on most occasions, perhaps making for a gruelling session. However, it is the only way that any player can realistically hope to beat both the opposition and the house cut.

Above: A waitress serves poker players at Binion's casino. With food and drink constantly on offer during play, casinos do have ways other than gambling to extract money from visitors' pockets. The casino environment is geared towards cutting you off from the outside world and the level of concentration required to play well is difficult to sustain for long. It is advisable to regulate your time at the table and take regular breaks for refreshment.

Left: Among the signature attractions at Caesar's Palace hotel-casino, located on the Las Vegas Strip between the Bellagio and the Mirage, is the Colosseum theatre, where Céline Dion and Elton John have been regular performers. It was specifically built for the Dion show, *A New Day*, a spectacular produced by former Cirque du Soleil director Franco Dragone. Despite having some of the highest ticket prices for any show in the city, with seats as high as US$200 each, the show regularly sold out.

Right: To win when playing in poker games where the house takes a cut, a player must not only beat opponents, but also the financial drain of the rake. The rake represents a fee for the facilities, and it's also customary to tip the dealer when you win the pot. So even a winning session does not come without some expense.

Games and facilities

The poker variations on offer in casinos tend to reflect current trends, with Texas Hold 'em, seven-card stud and Omaha most prominent, although other games are generally available on request. The split-pot and low-only games such as Omaha/8, razz, lowball and seven-card stud/8 are also popular, although not as widely available. Larger establishments sometimes offer separate rates for a private room or table at which players may engage in whichever game they choose. Typically, hiring such a facility is usually conditional on it being in use for a minimum of, perhaps, six hours.

Aside from poker, of course, casinos offer many other gambling facilities that have proved the downfall of many successful poker players. Even the late Stu Ungar, three times a world champion, had a reputation for leaving a casino broke on occasions, despite having won substantial sums at the poker table. In terms of ancillary services, players will often find themselves waited on while playing poker, since staff will be on hand to take orders for drinks and perhaps even food. Play for long enough and there is a chance that complimentary refreshments will be offered, but this service is not universally available.

Above: One of several slot machine halls inside the Golden Nugget casino-hotel. Casinos operate to make money and they are generally very good at it. Given that the space occupied by one poker table could easily accommodate perhaps a dozen machines, simple economics have contributed to the game being marginalized by casinos in the past.

AVIATION CLUB DE FRANCE, PARIS
♦ ♣ ♥ ♠

Situated at 10, Avenue de Champs-Elysées, the Aviation Club de France in Paris is regarded as one of the most stylish casinos in the world. It was established in 1907 primarily to cater for baccarat players but is now readily associated with poker courtesy of the Grand Prix de Paris, a Texas Hold 'em tournament that ranks among the most prestigious in Europe and constitutes part of the World Poker Tour. The card room offers a wide range of cash games including Omaha, seven-card stud and their high-low variations, along with Texas Hold 'em. It also boasts its own hybrid of Hold 'em in which players are dealt four cards, one of which must be discarded before the flop while a second must be mucked before the turn card is revealed. Buying in to a game can cost from €50 to €10,000 and the betting structures, starting at €2/€4 for fixed-limit tables, vary according to the minimum buy-in but include fixed-, pot- and no-limit games. Daily €50 no-limit Hold 'em tournaments are staged each morning and afternoon, and on Saturday evenings there is a similar event for which the buy-in is €250. In common with many of Europe's prominent casinos, the Aviation Club insists that its patrons dress smartly, declining to admit anyone wearing a t-shirt or trainers.

THE PLAYERS

While the number of regular players who attend a home game may vary, in a casino the likelihood is that cash game tables will have from seven to ten players at a time competing against each other. If this represents a greater number of opponents than an individual is used to facing, then it is worth remembering that a more conservative approach will be required to garner any success. This is particularly important when bearing in mind that some of these opponents may be very good players indeed, added to which the house rake is an ever-present obstacle to negotiate. The standard of opposition very much depends on the location of the poker room, the stake levels in operation and, perhaps, even the time of day chosen to play. Peak times tend to be during the evenings and at weekends, of course, when games are likely to represent far tougher propositions.

Pros, semi-pros and tourists

The nature of the opposition varies from one card room to another, so a little research is advisable when considering a visit to a commercial establishment. Online reviews of specific venues can help players identify those that may best suit their financial means and skills. This is certainly a useful tool for anyone thinking of playing in Las Vegas or Atlantic City, although not all locations are as saturated with poker rooms as these hotbeds of tourism.

Wherever a player's chosen card room is situated, the likelihood is that there will be a regular clientele for whom poker is a major source of income. Such professionals, given their experience, will normally play at the higher-stakes tables, but they can be found playing lower-stakes cash games too. They may be passing the time waiting for a seat at a bigger game to

Above: Many of the largest hotel, casino and resort properties in the world are located on 'The Strip'– four miles of boulevard that has been designated an All-American Road. New casinos design their facades to attract walk-up customers and many of these entrances have become attractions themselves.

Left: Professional Danish poker player Mads Andersen, winner of the four-day EPT Scandinavian Open 2006, which saw him take home €341,000 in winnings. The Dane had to work hard for the money, with the final table lasting a record 10 hours. Before making his mark in the poker world, Andersen was a former World Backgammon Champion.

become available or, having endured a run of bad fortune, may be trying to restore their bankroll by capitalizing on the inexperience of casual players. Such tourists commonly make the mistake of playing a little too loosely in their eagerness to become involved in the action, perhaps replicating the style of play in their regular home games. By trying to force the issue in this fashion, inexperienced players make the task of the patient professionals and semi-professionals that much easier. The latter will know that by waiting for a top-quality hand before betting, they will almost certainly find a caller or two who is immediately at a disadvantage and so likely to lose the pot.

Anybody considering a poker holiday of some form, particularly to Las Vegas, should approach the experience with a realistic set of expectations. The prospect of an average player winning a fortune at the poker table is unlikely given the typical standard of competition. Indeed, conventional wisdom suggests that poker tourists should budget for losses at the table as they would for any other leisure entertainment. Anyone who breaks even over a few sessions while managing to combat the ravages of the rake can then be satisfied that they have skills of a competent player.

Above: Tourists enjoying the nightlife in Las Vegas, marketed as 'the entertainment capital of the world', also commonly known as 'sin city' due to the popularity of legalized gambling, availability of alcohol at any time, and various forms of adult entertainment. The city's image has made it a popular setting for films and television programmes.

Below: Increasing numbers of casinos offer table card games where there are alternative ways to play and win. Three card poker is an exciting stud poker game where players may bet against the dealer or bet on the value of their own three-card hand or bet both. Bonus payouts may be had for certain wagers against the dealer.

CONCORD CARD CASINO, VIENNA
♦ ♣ ♥ ♠

The Concord Card Casino, located on the Geiselbergstrasse in Vienna, has only been open since 1993 and boasted Europe's largest poker room until the opening of the UK's Dusk till Dawn club in 2007. No-limit Texas Hold 'em, pot-limit Omaha and fixed-limit seven-card stud account for the bulk of the games played, with the casino acknowledging that many more young players are taking seats at its 30 poker tables. Fixed-limit Hold 'em is also on offer at stakes of €3/€6 and above, while seven-card stud games are available on request. Tournaments are organized each evening with buy-ins from €24.

The Concord stages several high-stakes tournaments during the year, the most prestigious being the Austrian Poker Championship, part of Vienna's Spring Poker Festival held in March, and the European Poker Masters. Both competitions require a buy-in of €3,000. The Concord has no membership policy although it insists that players dress relatively smartly and do not wear jeans or t-shirts.

THE CASINO ENVIRONMENT

Casino profitability is dependent upon keeping customers comfortably entertained for as long as possible, since the longer they stay, the more likely it is that they will lose money. Windows and clocks are noticeable by their absence and, with air-conditioning systems that help maintain a constant temperature, the whole casino experience is geared towards separating clients from any connection with the outside world.

Poker players may benefit from preferential facilities in some establishments, but many poker rooms compete for space with other gambling attractions. Consequently, it is quite common for a busy room with plenty of tables in operation to generate a great volume of noise, which, along with the distractions emanating from other gaming tables, can test a player's powers of concentration. Technological developments have seen the larger, more prestigious poker rooms striving to improve their booking systems in an effort to help operations run more smoothly, but regular poker players can be tough customers to please.

Playing conditions

Anyone seriously contemplating a game of poker normally expects to spend several hours engaged in competition, even if moving from one table to another during a session. With this in mind, the conditions of play with regard to the poker room itself become more significant. The large oval tables could host ten players who are all sat in close proximity to each other, which, if the scene is replicated throughout the room, can make the experience slightly claustrophobic. If this in itself is not too intimidating, then confronting opponents wearing hats or sunglasses to obscure their facial expressions may seem slightly disconcerting. In terms of physical well-being, an occasional break from even the most comfortable seat will be needed and poker rooms with toilet facilities nearby always score highly with reviewers.

At the tables, competent dealers will ensure a steady pace to the game, with some venues even possessing automatic shuffling machines to help reduce the inevitable pause between hands. There will rarely be time for players to indulge in a weighty discussion on the outcome of a hand before the next is dealt, such inquests being of little interest to those who were not involved, in any case.

Above: American Russ Hamilton receiving a massage during the Hold 'em main event in the 2005 World Series of Poker. Hamilton, who started playing poker when he was seven, won in 1994, claiming a US$1 million prize. Since it was the 25th anniversary, he also won his weight in silver.

Above: Inside the Casino Barrière de Deauville, France, during the French Open tournament of 2005. In the annals of James Bond history, it is said that Ian Fleming, the spy's creator, modelled the gambling salon of his novel *Casino Royale* on the baize tables and spinning roulette wheels in Deauville.

Distractions

Coming to terms with an unfamiliar environment, speed of play at the table and the quality of the opposition is a major challenge, given the other potential distractions in a card room. It can be difficult to ignore the general level of background noise arising from adjacent tables and the steady stream of players coming and going from the facility. Also, spectators may sometimes stop by to see how play is progressing, either because they are checking out the competition at a table for which they would like a seat or, perhaps, because they are friendly with one of the players competing in the game. If waiting staff are on hand to provide table service as well, the potential level of disruption to a player's concentration becomes apparent.

Coping with these factors is a test of character, of course, but if a player feels uncomfortable at any time, it is always best to take a break or change tables if possible. Anything that creates a degree of stress while playing is bound to have an impact on an individual's performance, which will inevitably detract from the experience of playing in a dedicated poker room.

TRUMP TAJ MAHAL, ATLANTIC CITY
♦ ♣ ♥ ♠

Recently voted 'best casino' by *Casino Player* magazine readers, the Trump Taj Mahal boasts Atlantic City's biggest poker room and has played host to the US Poker Championships for the past 10 years. Tables are dedicated to Texas Hold 'em, Omaha and seven-card stud, along with their high-low variants, and there are free daily lessons teaching newcomers. Stake levels begin at US$1/$3 for seven-card stud and US$2/$4 for pot-limit Texas Hold 'em, while there are no-limit Texas Hold 'em tournaments staged each day. The minimum buy-in is for US$50 plus US$15, and the events start at various times during the day, with the betting levels rising every 20 minutes. Opened in 1990 and built to rival anything on offer in Las Vegas, the Trump Taj Mahal is a major attraction for holidaymakers, as well as poker tourists, drawn to the east coast of America.

Above: The trademark sunglasses that professional poker player Greg Raymer wore when he won the 2004 World Series of Poker tournament. The holographic lizard eyes began as a joke during a big hand in the 2002 WSOP, but it seemed to have a desirable effect, distracting his opponent. Since then, Raymer has worn the glasses in all the major poker tournaments that he has played.

Right: A lit fountain shimmers at night in front of a large neon sign at the Trump Taj Mahal casino resort in Atlantic City. It is currently undergoing a US$250 million renovation and addition of a new hotel tower, on which work commenced in July 2006.

KEY ADVICE

Putting into practice the principles outlined so far is always going to be difficult the first time a player tackles casino poker. However, while it may take a while to adjust to the different conditions, there are several key factors worth remembering that can help alleviate any initial stress. Perhaps the most obvious is to choose a game at a comfortable stake level that is relative to the size of a player's bankroll. If successfully adopting a more cautious attitude, it is possible that a player could see the deal circulate the table several times before winning a hand. Having sufficient chips to cover the antes or blinds while, perhaps, losing the odd contested pot is therefore essential to enable a player to sustain interest throughout such a lean spell.

Should a game at the right level not be available, then it is better to play for lower stakes, rather than joining a game that is, in all conscience, beyond one's means. A profitable session against players of similar ability might provide the impetus to move up a grade, and this situation is certainly more likely to enhance a player's confidence than dropping down a level, having already lost a substantial chunk of one's bankroll. Understanding the routines of a chosen poker variation is also vital, of course, since playing an unfamiliar game is likely to prove a costly exercise in education without some prior knowledge of even the most basic strategies to adopt.

Above: Edgar Skjervold at the EPT Monte Carlo event in 2006. Skjervold, a 30-year-old financial analyst from Oslo, Norway, is part of a group of Norwegian players who have burst upon the poker scene in recent years. He shot to prominence after winning the World Championship of Online Poker in 2004, taking home US$424,945, the largest internet cash prize in history.

Above: A tired-looking actor Tobey Maguire reacting to losing during a game of Texas Hold 'em at the World Series of Poker in Las Vegas in 2005. Casinos are designed to shake cash from your pockets and can wear you down if you do not take regular breaks. Exhausted players would do well to remember that a game will always be happening somewhere tomorrow.

Budgeting time

Presented with an opportunity to play poker at any time, day or night, it is easy for players to fall into the trap of over-indulging their interest. Maintaining the levels of concentration required to play studiously and competently is a tall order for even the most accomplished professionals. Knowing when to walk away from the table is therefore as much a part of disciplined poker play as anything a player may need to exhibit while in competition. One lapse in concentration could undo plenty of good work earlier in the session, so regular breaks are also advisable when intending to play for several hours at a time.

This is particularly important if, having played well, an individual suffers a bad beat that wipes out any short-term gains already accrued. Controlling the anger or frustration experienced following an unlucky loss can test the mettle of almost any player, but only the very best are able to accept the result calmly and not allow it to prejudice their subsequent betting patterns. The crucial thing to

Right: Chips from the Grosvenor Victoria casino. A highlight of The Vic's poker calendar is the annual Grosvenor Grand Prix, an event which features a collection of big buy-in tournaments and attracts players from all over Europe to compete for millions of pounds in prize money.

Left: Among the largest and oldest of the casinos in the UK, 'The Vic', as it is known, featured a classic upset during The Poker Classics, held there in April 2005, when the relatively unknown Andy Church placed first among nearly two hundred players, including many who are well known on the circuit.

avoid in such circumstances is the type of reckless play that signifies a player is 'on tilt' – this is characterized by betting more heavily on marginal hands to try and compensate for earlier perceived injustices. Should any player suspect that their game is deteriorating along these lines, it is well worth remembering that a fresh opportunity to play is rarely long in coming, such is the widespread access to poker now available.

GROSVENOR VICTORIA CASINO, LONDON
♦ ♣ ♥ ♠

London's Grosvenor Victoria Casino, often referred to as 'The Vic', is a popular haunt for many of the city's top poker players and it regularly stages high-stakes tournaments, some occasionally recorded for television. Its two card rooms offer 20 poker tables and there are daily no-limit Texas Hold 'em tournaments at stake levels ranging from £30, plus administration fees. Inexpensive rebuy tournaments for beginners are a feature of Friday nights and such games are an increasingly common part of the casino scene, such is the demand for the game in the UK. Anyone wishing to enter the Grosvenor Victoria will have to register for free membership by producing some form of personal identification. However, players are permitted to enter the premises promptly, having registered, rather than being forced to wait for 24 hours before sampling the action, as was the case until the UK removed this legal stipulation in 2005. Along with most of the country's casinos, a 'smart casual' dress code is *de rigeur*.

Above: English Roland 'the Sheep' de Wolfe at the final table of the EPT event in Dublin in 2006. He went on to win the tournament and the top prize of €554,300 (US$737,208) in the no-limit Texas Hold 'em event.

Above: The final table during the European Poker Tour's second season held in London in October 2005 at the Grosvenor Victoria Casino. American Noah Jefferson and Norwegian Jonas Helness watch as British player Mark Teltscher checks his cards. Teltscher went on to win the £3,000 (US$5,900) no-limit Hold 'em main event, taking home £280,000 (US$552,000).

Cash Games and Tournaments

As a gambling medium, poker has always been premised upon the idea of players vying with each other for sums of cash or some other meaningful currency. Since its early days, however, poker has developed into a wide range of different games with a variety of betting structures to match. Up until the 1970s, poker remained conceptually a cash game, with players buying in for a stipulated maximum or minimum sum prior to a session. But the success of the WSOP and the exposure of poker on television have increased the popularity of tournament poker, which has also been given a phenomenal boost by the advent of online gambling sites. This has led to distinctive differences in the strategies and approaches to be adopted when playing cash game poker as opposed to a tournament. The purpose of this chapter is to identify some of those differences and outline the key facets of both forms of the game.

Right: A player rakes in the chips at the conclusion of a hand. Whether playing a cash game or a tournament, winning a hand and claiming the pot is every player's objective as the cards are being dealt. Those new to the game often mistakenly believe that winning at poker is predicated upon winning a majority of hands played during a session. Experienced players know, however, that the key to long-term success lies in winning the few hands that generate big pots. This holds true for both cash games and poker tournaments even if strategies applied in one form of the game may not always be advisable in the other.

Cash Games

Cash games, or ring games if preferred, are the mainstay of poker and involve players gambling with the money at their disposal, usually in the form of chips obtained from the acting cashier. The stake levels and betting limits of the various games differ, of course, and players will naturally gravitate towards those that suit them best.

Typically, in a formal card room, there will be a minimum buy-in required of perhaps as little as five times the maximum bet, offering the scope for playing at minimal cost. However, most experts recommend that players should not consider sitting in on any game with less than forty times the maximum bet. This is premised on the assumption that any fulfilling poker session will most probably last for several hours during which time a sustained run of poor cards or bad beats is almost inevitable.

In games where a maximum buy-in also applies, players may be allowed to rebuy chips during a pause in play to maintain their stacks at that level. Taking advantage of this possibility is also advised as a very positive strategy for two reasons. First, under table-stakes rules, players can only bet with the chips currently on the table, with any rebuys to be conducted at the conclusion of the hand. Betting all-in when holding the nuts is much more profitable with a large stack than with a small one, should a big pot develop, therefore it makes sense to keep as many chips as possible available for such an eventuality. This obviously involves avoiding games in which the buy-in could immediately absorb a player's entire bankroll. The second reason for doing so is simply to maintain a credible defence against opponents who bet aggressively to intimidate those short on chips. Without the

Above: Actor Lou Diamond Phillips playing poker at the Celebrity World Poker Tour held at the Commerce Casino in Los Angeles, USA. A popular spectator sport, celebrity poker has many actors among its leading lights. The cash winnings are often donated to charity.

Left: Rhett Butler (Clark Gable) keeps a cool head while playing poker in the film of *Gone with the Wind*. In real life too, containing one's emotions is an essential part of playing the game well.

resources to make the occasional re-raise, players run the risk of being anted away in the face of aggressive betting while they are waiting for a competitive hand. It is difficult to be successful if, when such as hand is held, a player does not have the resources to capitalize upon it to the fullest extent.

The long-term strategy

Although poker is rooted in competition, the risks that must be taken in order to win will very often lead to defeat. This applies during every hand of every session, which means that players must very quickly come to terms with losing and how it can affect their decisions. Having the discipline to control one's emotional reactions while playing poker is an asset, since it is all too easy to tilt, following a succession of losing hands. By allowing frustration or anger to guide one's play, it is likely that any losses will be compounded by poor betting decisions. Not every session will prove profitable and being able to walk away from the table while losing is a test of character that confronts every poker player.

Such a prospect is easier to accept when each individual session is considered merely one of countless others to be played during a lifetime. By setting realistic targets and keeping a record of performances, regular players who hope to improve their game, and perhaps even make it profitable, are better able to put losing sessions into perspective.

THE BANKROLL
♦ ♣ ♥ ♠

Managing the bankroll is of the utmost importance for a poker player, this being the cash specifically reserved for playing the game. Very few poker players are sponsored and the majority of full-time professionals are entirely reliant upon their ability to win in order to earn an income. Should their bankroll become exhausted, they have no immediate means of buying in to another game, which is one of the reasons why the best players are ruthless and clinical in their approach; they cannot afford to adopt any other attitude. Most players, however, will simply allocate a proportion of their income to poker in much the same way as they would for any other leisure interest. For the amateur, the test of discipline comes in treating the bankroll in the same way as a professional, since that is the surest way of promoting a competitive instinct.

ADOPTING THE RIGHT APPROACH

The reasons for playing poker are as many and varied as the people who enjoy the game, although purists insist that players should always strive to be as tough, ruthless and competitive as possible in order to do themselves justice. Each individual may have contrasting motives for playing, but all should consider some basic questions concerning how long they may wish to play, the nature of the opposition, and the potential cost involved. Only when these questions are satisfactorily answered can they hope to feel at ease and ready to play their best. Similarly, approaching the game in a positive frame of mind is obviously advantageous, with players who are tired, jaded or otherwise distracted by external pressures unlikely to exploit their true ability.

Home games

Regular games conducted at home between friends or colleagues have the potential to be as harshly competitive as any casino session involving poker's high-rollers. On the whole, though, such games are typically social events played for sums that are rarely large enough to endanger long-lasting friendships. Food, drink and conversation are as much a part of such events as playing cards, and this should be taken into account when devising even the vaguest of strategies.

Winning may not be the most pressing concern for the amateur player but nobody deliberately sets out to lose. Observing opponents to gather an appreciation of their playing styles and levels of ability remains an important skill. This is particularly true when invited to play in a regular home game for the first time, since even good friends may reveal personal characteristics in their poker that had previously never surfaced during the relationship.

Clubs and casinos

Buying in to a table operated by a club or casino can be a daunting experience for the novice player who is better acquainted with the home game. Although the stake levels may offer clues regarding the ability of the opposition, engaging in competition with strangers still requires a degree of self-confidence in one's own skill. Choosing the correct level at which to play is crucial, of course, and a disciplined approach to the time that is to be spent playing during a session is also important. Also, in formal card rooms there is always the rake to consider, this being the fee levied by the house for operating the game. The fee could be charged on an hourly basis, either per table or per player, or it could simply be that the dealer takes a few

Above: The home is where most poker is played. Using chips brings credibility to the game. Apart from being easier to use than cash, they help speed up the action.

Right: Extreme Poker is an initiative that is taking the game to exhilarating frontiers, no matter how strange. Poker professional Rob Varkonyi (far left) competes against other players during the second Extreme Poker tournament, held atop the vast ice fields of the Arctic Sea in Kemi, Finland, in March 2006.

chips from every winning pot up to a maximum of perhaps 10 per cent. With a cut from each pot going to the house and the winner of each reasonable pot customarily tipping the dealer, the pace of the game will also be quicker than in home games, it being in the dealer's interests to ensure that is the case. The combination of all these factors underlines, once more, the need for a realistic assessment of one's ability when deciding to play in public.

Quality of opponents

Players can expect to encounter opponents of much higher quality in commercial card rooms than they would in their home games. Leaving aside the tournament-level professionals, many other players manage to grind out a living from poker, defying the rake and their opponents in order to do it. For these players and the semi-professionals who supplement their regular income with profitable stints at the table, poker is simply a job requiring a high degree of application. Those they prey upon are the tourists, occasional poker players whose bankrolls, perhaps, exceed their abilities but who enjoy the chance to pit their wits against the best. Although it is a much more impersonal experience, the same considerations still apply for those who play online.

KEEPING COUNT
♦ ♣ ♥ ♠

So much advice concerning sound poker play emphasizes the benefits of analysing performance, as well as exercising discipline and patience. These virtues are also important for the serious player who wishes to improve with experience. Keeping a mental record of one's play in certain scenarios is an asset when studying the game away from the table. Players should also keep accurate financial records of their poker. Ultimately, money is simply a means of keeping score, with a good poker player being one who, year after year, regularly makes a profit. Only by being honest with themselves and making an accurate note of poker income and expenditure can players expect to be objective about their overall performance.

Left: It can be argued that the televising of poker tournaments has already given poker playing a whole new air of respectability, which is sure to attract a lot of people to try it.

TOURNAMENT PLAY

Inspired by television coverage of tournament poker and the potential prize money on offer for winning, many more players are developing a taste for this form of the game. Whereas a commercial cash game in a 24-hour club or casino may, in theory, continue indefinitely as players come and go from the table, a tournament is structured to ensure a definitive winner at the end of the event. To this end, the antes and blinds in tournaments progressively increase, whereas in cash poker, they remain at a constant level as dictated by the terms of the game. Each betting level may apply for a matter of minutes or a matter of hours, depending on the nature and scale of the tournament, but the principle is always the same, with the objective for each player, of course, being to win all the chips in play.

Knockout poker

The major difference between cash games and tournaments is, of course, the knockout element that sees players eliminated when they run out of chips. To last the distance, players are compelled to engage in betting confrontations, which means they have to implement different strategies and contrasting styles of play at the various stages of the tournament.

In a cash game, tight players can usually allow the deal to circulate the table a couple of times while waiting for a playable hand, without the antes seriously damaging their chip stacks. Although commendable as a general long-term playing strategy, the nature of knockout poker precludes maintaining this patient approach throughout a tournament. During the early stages, when survival is of primary concern, patience is certainly required, but, as the antes increase and opponents acquire more chips, players must bet forcefully and be prepared to take greater risks.

Above: American Joe Bartholdi, winner of the 2006 WPT no-limit Hold 'em US$25,000 buy-in championship sits amid bundles of cash after winning US$3.7 million – the biggest pot ever in the tournament's history up to that point. Bartholdi outlasted a field of 605 players to claim the first place prize. The victory came after years of mixed fortunes due to experiencing difficulty maintaining a stable bankroll.

Left: An enormous poster for Full Tilt Poker, found outside the game room at the 2005 WSOP. The online gaming site is well known for having a huge team of poker professionals on its advertising team (Phil Ivey, Chris 'Jesus' Ferguson, Howard Lederer, Mike Matusow, to name but a few). The site has excellent reviews for its software: its website was designed by professional players. Full Tilt's advertising campaigns have taken promotion of the game to a new level.

Entry fees and prize structures

For tournaments, entry fees vary dramatically, with the events held at the WSOP, for example, generally costing US$500 and upwards, while the World Championship game itself requires a buy-in of US$10,000. At the lower end of the scale, casinos and clubs stage tournaments for much smaller entry fees and such games are also a very popular element of online poker. There are even freeroll tournaments that require no entry fee but usually result in the winner being offered a seat in a more prestigious competition. Satellite tournaments are similar in nature, with players paying a small fee for the chance to win a place in the next round of the main event.

The great benefit of playing tournament poker compared to cash games is that players can be certain at the outset of the maximum they stand to lose. In order to win, however, it is possible they may have to outlast several hundred opponents, which is obviously a major challenge. The prize money is usually allocated to those who finish in the top ten per cent of entrants, but the lion's share of the cash tends to be reserved for the top three or four per cent, the winner perhaps claiming between a quarter and a half of the entire prize pool.

Types of tournament

Most of the popular variations are played in tournament fashion and all can be conducted as fixed-pot or no-limit contests. The number of competitors may range from the 8,000-strong entry for the WSOP World Championship, the most celebrated of all multi-table tournaments, to a private heads-up contest between just two players. Single-table tournaments exist that offer players a better chance of victory for a much smaller top prize, of course, and many of these are known as sit 'n' go events. Players simply pay the required fee and, when all seats are taken, the tournament immediately begins. These differ from the regular diarized competitions for which players may enter some time in advance.

One other key factor for players to bear in mind is the distinction between freeze-out and rebuy tournaments. In the former, all players start with the same number of chips for their fixed fee and play until they either lose them all or win the tournament. Subject to certain conditions, players may purchase more chips during a rebuy tournament, with the opportunity to do this typically restricted to the first hour or two of the event. After that, the tournament continues as a freeze-out competition.

Above left: Eventual winner of the WSOP 2006 championship, Jamie Gold (centre), focuses on a hand as the players compete to be in the final nine. It stands to reason that at this stage, players must be observant in order to pick up clues from the table. The prospect of reaching the final table beckons, and with it a share of the prize pool, so players may tighten up their play to protect their chip position.

Left: Pack of cards on display at the WSOP championship in 2004. Like any major sporting event, the WSOP has corporate sponsors which pay fees to market themselves as an official sponsor or licensee and exclusively use the WSOP insignia and cross-promote with their events. In addition to Harrah's properties and cable TV networks dedicated to sports broadcasting, the major sponsors have included Miller Brewing, Pepsi, GlaxoSmithKline/Bayer and Nintendo.

TOURNAMENT STRATEGY

A single-table event with rapidly increasing betting levels may be over in a matter of minutes, while most multi-table tournaments comprising thirty or more entrants could easily last for several hours. The likely duration of the tournament will therefore have a bearing on strategy, as only those who finish in the top ten per cent typically win a share of the prize pool.

During the early stages, survival is very much the primary concern and players are advised to adopt a tight and cautious approach while they evaluate the opposition. Judgement of starting hands is crucial and, whichever poker variation is being played, avoiding unnecessary and potentially costly confrontations early on in the tournament is generally advisable. There will always be those who prefer to gamble from the outset, in an attempt to gain an early advantage, but playing a conservative game while reckless opponents knock each other out is arguably a better long-term strategy.

Having evaded an early exit, however, players can still expect the pressure to build as the tournament develops. The regular increases in the minimum betting level ensure this as players find themselves having to contest pots with hands they might ordinarily fold. Those who are short of chips can expect to see large and intimidating bets emanating from the chip leaders as the proximity of the prize-money places draws near.

Distinguishing features

Recognizing distinctive betting patterns among opponents is always important at the poker table. This is no less true in a tournament and is an asset at a single-table event in which players only vacate their seats when they are eliminated. Distinguishing the cautious strategists from the loose gamblers is relatively straightforward under these circumstances.

Multi-table tournaments present a different challenge, however, since players will be moved between tables, to equalize numbers as others are

Above: British player Arshad Hussain, at the EPT 2006 grand final held in Monte Carlo. The dramatic final stages of the tournament ended with Hussain in a heads-up showdown against American political science student Jeff Williams, who went on to win the big event taking home €900,000 (US$1,078,000). Arshad had spent nothing to reach Monte Carlo after winning an online satellite tournament and took home €492,000 (US$592,607) for his second place.

Left: Players try their luck during the early stages of the WSOP 2006 held at the Rio hotel and casino, in Las Vegas. The enormous scale of the tournament can be intimidating for amateur players, and ten- or eleven-handed games mean that space at tables is tight.

Left: Players at the WSOP 2006 final table. As has become customary at the final table of WSOP events, the prize money is brought out by armed security guards and put on display. The previously unknown American player Jamie Gold completely dominated the table and went on to win US$12 million without ever being seriously challenged.

Below: 'Diamond' Carlo Citrone, British professional poker player and commentator, enjoys a massage at the table during the 2005 World Series of Poker where he made it to the final table. Citrone ultimately collected US$59,175 in cash for coming 8th out of a total of 1,072 players.

eliminated and tables are taken out of action. Having acquired a healthy chip lead at one table and profited from the opportunity to intimidate the short stacks, a player could be moved to another table where an opponent or two may have many more chips. If this is the case, a player once again needs to take stock of the opposition and their betting styles to discover whether the leaders have been skilfully shrewd or simply lucky. Of course, as the tournament progresses towards the final table and the antes or blinds increase, betting patterns tend to be dictated by the chips at a player's disposal more than any other factor.

Monitoring chip stacks

The need to keep abreast of developments elsewhere is an element of multi-table tournament play that is not replicated in cash games. The technology behind online tournaments facilitates hand-by-hand updates, allowing contestants to gauge their progress against opponents at other tables. Outside the world of the virtual casino, however, players may have to take the occasional break from their own game in order to regroup their thoughts and check the progress of opponents at other tables.

In a freeze-out contest, the total number of chips in play is constant, so calculating the current average is a straightforward matter of dividing the chip total by the number of players remaining. Maintaining an

above-average chip stack during the earlier stages of a tournament can provide the foundation for more attacking play as short-stacked opponents are threatened by the prospect of elimination. However, it is worth remembering that from the middle stages onwards, the average stack may be some way short of the chip leader if one player has managed to attain a dominant lead.

How to Win

The greater the number of competitors, the more difficult any tournament is to win, of course, and it is true that players may have to rely on good fortune at key moments to a greater extent than when contesting a cash game. Armed with a sound strategy and a consistent approach in the selection of which hands to support, players are more likely to finish ahead on a regular basis if restricting their poker to the cash game format.

Tournament poker, however, calls for more risks to be taken in order both to survive and to prosper. The size of a player's chip stack will dictate the frequency and scale of those risks, with players who are down to ten times the minimum bet or less faced with the prospect that every hand could be their last. Those in good shape have more options from which to choose, since they can contest a few more multi-handed pots with low-ranking cards if opponents choose not to raise the betting. Alternatively, there is always the option to sit back for a while and wait patiently while opponents jostle for position by eliminating each other. Anyone who has improved on their starting stack by judiciously sticking to a tight game plan is also in a better position to bluff from the middle stages onwards as the cost of participating in a hand inevitably increases. Opponents will be wary of calling such a solid player and this provides the opportunity to pick up some valuable chips from some weakly contested pots.

Stay alert

The key to absorbing all the information available while playing poker is concentration, whatever form of the game is being played. In tournaments, taking stock of the opposition, their playing styles and the fluctuations in stack sizes requires a high degree of mental application. Accomplishing this as well as monitoring events at the surrounding tables demands that competitors stay alert. As the average chip count increases, for example, players should be acutely aware that they need to win a few pots to stay ahead of the game. The danger with playing too tightly and falling well behind is that a player may eventually face betting all-in with such limited resources that even winning the hand may be of little benefit. Being alert to the possibility of this happening and adjusting one's play accordingly can therefore prevent a player from having to implement increasingly desperate strategies.

Above: In 2006, British newspaper columnist, author and TV presenter Victoria Cohen beat 397 others to win £500,000 (US$976,200) in the EPT event in London.

Above: Former investment banker Rob Varkonyi winning the WSOP in 2002. The American became a celebrity and professional poker player after his surprise victory. Phil Hellmuth said that the odds against Varkonyi winning were so high that he would shave his head if he won.

Above: Norwegian Bjorn-Erik Glenne was crowned winner of the European Poker Tour event in Barcelona in 2006, beating 480 players to claim the €691,000 prize (US$875,000). The former marketing manager is the first Norwegian to win an EPT event. Glenne is also a high-ranking chess player and enjoys substantial success online.

Left: Chris Moneymaker at the final table of the 2003 WSOP. He earned his way into the championship event by playing in an online poker tournament at a cost of US$40 and went on to win the first prize of US$2.5 million, despite the fact it was his first experience of a 'live' poker tournament.

From the chip leader's perspective, choosing the right time to pressurize a short-stacked opponent is no less challenging. While intimidating the opposition with large bets is a viable option, it is still best to do so when in possession of a strong hand. Inducing all-in calls or raises from opponents short on chips can easily backfire if betting with a marginal hand, since being vulnerable does not preclude them from having excellent cards. Similarly, calling a short-stacked opponent's all-in bet is easier to justify when holding a decent hand, there being little profit from continually calling in such situations simply because one has the chips to spare.

Change gear

The ability to change gear by varying one's betting patterns and general approach is required in both cash games and tournaments. In the former, adopting a contrasting style to that prevalent among the opposition can be beneficial, with tight play best at a table of loose players, and more expansive play possible when the opposition is ultra-conservative.

Responding in a similar way during a tournament is a good policy in the early stages, but the need to change gear is dictated by the increasing betting levels and the unavoidable impact they have on each competitor's play. Acquiring chips to withstand the ravages of the antes and blinds means players will often have to contemplate betting with a poor hand. Taking a positive stance and betting aggressively in this situation is generally a better policy than passively calling and hoping for the best. Having to adopt this more forceful approach on occasions is probably the greatest distinguishing factor between tournaments and cash games, where a consistently patient strategy can prove rewarding. As a result, individuals who regularly play tournament poker should adjust their thinking accordingly when reverting to a cash game.

INDEX

BIBLIOGRAPHY

Alvarez, Al, *The Biggest Game in Town* (Houghton Mifflin, Boston, 1983)

Bellin, Andy, *Poker Nation: A High-Stakes, Low-Life Adventure into the Heart of Gambling* (Yellow Jersey Press, London, 2003)

Brunson, Doyle, *Doyle Brunson's Super System: A Course in Power Poker* (B & G Publishing, Las Vegas, 1978)

Dalla, Nolan, and Alson, Peter, *The Man Behind the Shades: The Rise and Fall of Stuey 'The Kid' Ungar, Poker's Greatest Player* (Phoenix, London, 2006)

Fletcher, Iain, *The Rough Guide to Poker* (Rough Guides Ltd, London, 2005)

Hellmuth Jr, Phil, *Play Poker Like the Pros* (HarperCollins, New York, 2003)

Marcus, Richard, *The Great Casino Heist* (Constable & Robinson Ltd, London, 2005)

McEoy, Tom, *Tournament Poker* (Cardoza, New York, 1995)

McNally, Brian, *How to Play Poker and Win* (Macmillan, London, 2000)

Scarne, John, *Scarne's Guide to Modern Poker* (Pocket Books, New York, 1980)

Sklansky, David, *Hold 'em Poker* (Two Plus Two Publishing LLC, Henderson, 1978)

Steiner, Peter O., *Thursday-Night Poker: How to Understand, Enjoy – and Win* (Random House, New York, 1996)

Wilson, Des, *Swimming with the Devilfish…under the surface of professional poker* (Macmillan, London, 2006)

Wolpin, Stewart, *The Rules of Neighbourhood Poker According to Hoyle* (New Chapter Press, New York, 1990)

Yarnold, Stuart, *Online Poker in Easy Steps* (Computer Step, Southam, 2005)

Magazines & Periodicals

Inside Edge (Dennis Publishing, London)

Poker Player (Dennis Publishing, London)

WPT Poker: The Official World Poker Tour Magazine (Future Publishing, Bath)

Some Useful Poker Websites

www.askmen.com
www.blindbetpoker.com
www.doylesroom.com
www.homepoker.com
www.launchpoker.com
www.pagat.com
www.playwinningpoker.com
www.poker.com

www.pokernews.com
www.pokerplayernewspaper.com
www.pokersourceonline.com
www.pokertips.org
www.pokertop10.com
www.thehendonmob.com
www.usplayingcard.com
www.worldcasinodirectory.com

AUTHOR ACKNOWLEDGEMENTS

In order to bring this publication to fruition I have had to call upon the support of many people and I would like to take this opportunity to thank them personally for their help and advice. Firstly, I wish to recognize the hardworking contribution of the editorial team at Bridgewater Books, particularly Polita Caaveiro and Sarah Doughty, whose guidance has been of immense benefit. Also, I am indebted to Paul Turner at Broadcasting Dataservices Ltd for his support in helping me to find and manage the time needed to complete the project, and I thank him for his interest and encouragement during the months spent researching and writing the text. Thanks also to Adam, Chris, Warren, Roy, Maureen and Joasia for their help at a crucial time in the summer of 2006. Finally, I must also thank my wonderfully understanding partner, Gosia Pilak, for once again proving so patiently supportive while I spent vast quantities of time flirting with the demanding mistress that is the game of poker. Dziekuje bardzo, kochanie.

PICTURE CREDITS

The Publisher would like to thank the following for kindly supplying photographs for this book: **Alamy** 80 (b): **Corbis** 45 (bl), 58, 71 (bl), 79, 82, 92 (br), 105, 106 (b), 107 (t), 108 (br), 109 (t), 110 (bl), 111 (br), 116 (bl, br), 117 (tl), 120 (cr), 121 (cl); **Empics** 23, 93, 112 (tr), 118 (br), 122 (bl); **Getty** 18, 95 (tl), 100, 123 (tl); **Golden Nugget casino** 104 (bl), 107 (bl); **iStock Photography** 14, 15, 46, 48, 51, 53, 61, 65, 105 (t), 118 (bl); **The Kobal Collection Warner Bros** 60; **Photo library** 101 (cr), 109 (br); **Photos.com** 63; **Pokerimages.com** 44, 45 (tr), 71 (tr), 73, 104 (t), 106 (tr), 108 (bl), 110 (br), 111 (bl), 112 (b), 113 (tl, tr, bl, br), 117 (tr), 119 (br), 120 (bl), 122 (cr), 124 (bl, br), 125 (tl, tr);
www.pokerroom.com 92, 93; **www.pacificpoker.com** 94;
www.partypoker.com 94; **www.pokerstars.com** 94;
www.deutschepokertour.com 95; **www.pokerguide.jp** 96;
www.jeugapokerya.com 96; **www.redstarpoker.com** 96;
www.slo-poker.com 97; **www.poker.org.il** 97; **www.poker.com.hr** 98;
www.ecardroom.cn 98; **www.poker24.pl** 99; **www.spelapoker.se** 223;
www.poker.fr 99; **www.allaussiepoker.com** 101; **www.megapoker.nl** 101;
All other photos by Andrew Perris 6-7, 9, 13, 17, 19, 21, 24, 26, 27, 28, 32, 38, 35, 36, 37, 38, 39, 55, 57, 68, 80 (t), 81, 83, 85, 87, 90-91. 102-103, 114-115.

Every effort has been made to obtain permission to reproduce copyright material, but there may be cases where we have been unable to trace a copyright holder. The publisher will be happy to correct any omissions in future printings.

Odds Tables

Having an understanding of the odds and probabilities in poker is essential for anyone wishing to be successful at the game. It will give you a definite advantage over your opponents and help you work out your strategy for the rest of the game. Use the odds tables given here to decide on your play.

TEXAS HOLD 'EM: Odds Against Receiving Specific Starting Hands

Pair of Aces	220 to 1
Pair of Aces or Kings	119 to 1
Pair of Tens or better	43 to 1
Any Pair	16 to 1
Ace King suited	331 to 1
Ace King offsuit	110 to 1
Any two suited cards	3.25 to 1
Any hand with a pair or an Ace	4 to 1

SEVEN-CARD STUD: Odds Against Receiving Specific Starting Hands

Three Aces	5,524 to 1
Three Queens or better	1,841 to 1
Three Tens or better	1,104 to 1
Any three of a kind (Trips)	424 to 1
Pair of Aces	76 to 1
Pair of Queens or better	25 to 1
Pair of Tens or better	14 to 1
Three cards to a straight flush	85 to 1
Three cards to a flush	24 to 1
Three cards to a straight	5 to 1

DRAW POKER: Odds Against Improvement Following the Draw

Player Holds	Result	
One pair – draws three cards	Any improvement	5 to 2
	Two Pairs	5 to 1
	Three of a Kind (Trips)	8 to 1
	Full House	97 to 1
	Four of a Kind (Quads)	360 to 1
One pair plus a kicker – draws two cards	Any improvement	3 to 1
	Two Pairs	5 to
	Trips	12 to 1
	Full House	120 to 1
Two pairs – draws one card	Full House	11 to 1
Trips – draws two cards	Any improvement	9 to 1
	Full House	15 to 1
	Quads	23 to 1
Trips plus a kicker – draws one card	Any improvement	11 to 1
	Full House	15 to 1
	Quads	46 to 1
Open-ended straight draw – draws one card	Improvement to Straight	5 to 1
Inside straight draw – draws one card	Improvement to Straight	11 to 1
Four-card flush – draws one card	Improvement to Flush	4 to 1
Open-ended four-card straight flush – draws one card	Improvement to Straight Flush	23 to 1

TEXAS HOLD 'EM: On the Flop

Player holds	Result	
A Pair	Quads	407 to 1
	Full House	136 to 1
	Trips	7.5 to 1
Two unpaired cards	Full House	1087 to 1
	Trips	73 to 1
	Two Pairs (using both hole cards)	48 to 1
	Any Two Pairs	24 to 1
	Pair	2 to 1
Two suited cards	Flush completed	118 to 1
	Four-card Flush	7.5 to 1
	Three-card Flush	1.4 to 1